S0-BFO-527

IMITATION AND
OTHER ESSAYS

LONDON : HUMPHREY MILFORD

OXFORD UNIVERSITY PRESS

IMITATION
AND OTHER
ESSAYS

BY

CHARLES H. GRANDGENT

CAMBRIDGE

HARVARD UNIVERSITY PRESS

1933

WITHDRAWN
Eastern Oregon University
from EOU Library
1410 L Avenue
La Grande, OR 97850

COPYRIGHT, 1933
BY THE PRESIDENT AND FELLOWS OF
HARVARD COLLEGE

PRINTED AT THE HARVARD UNIVERSITY PRESS
CAMBRIDGE, MASS., U. S. A.

PREFACE

THE miscellaneous papers collected in this volume are all new to the press. The first, *Imitation*, is made up of two lectures given by me in February, 1931, at University College, London.

C. H. G.

JUNE, 1933

CONTENTS

Grandgent, Charles Hall. Imitation and other essays. Harvard
univ.; Lond. Oxford, 1933. 190p. $2.

Wit and a charming discursiveness mark
these essays, which begin with an affirmation,
entertainingly elaborated, to the effect that
philology is not a dull subject, and proceed
from academic topics to boyhood reminis-
cences. *Contents:* Imitation—Difficilior lectio
— Tee um lie — Behavior — Cracks in the
clouds—Out of antiquity—Old haunts.

814.5   33-32407

IMITATION AND
OTHER ESSAYS

IMITATION

Poetry and linguistics: how unrelated they seem nowadays to the lay mind! At opposite poles they lie in the accepted cosmogony of human creativeness. Often they are conceived as so antagonistic that they cannot abide, even at different periods, in one and the same mind. Many and many a graduate student in our universities may be heard to declare, with pathetic earnestness and still more pathetic reiteration, that he can never achieve the doctorate because, his tastes being altogether literary, he cannot bring himself to delve in "philology." "Philology" — by which he means the study of language itself, in its present state and in its successive stages — is a route reserved for prosy spirits, unfit to ride the winged horse. Even were he capable of pursuing it, the pursuit would in some fashion degrade him, would clip his wings and clog his feet, would drag him beneath the high level on which he dreams perpetually to perambulate. For he has the artist's temperament.

The artistic temperament possesses, to be sure, in many cases, but one symptom — an inborn disinclination to work. Yet by no means all the contemners of language — the stuff of which poetry is made — are idlers. A good proportion of them will unprotestingly submit to endless rehearsal of dates and titles, and to wearisome perusal of works (or summaries of works, or summaries of other people's summaries of works) written by fortuitously remembered poetasters who had better never have been born. In the matter of sheer difficulty, there would seem to be nothing to choose between the two disciplines. And on the score of human interest, why should a catalogue of literary incompetents offer more allurement than an attempt to follow the processes by which man has slowly forged for himself the implement of thought?

In reality, the protesters against linguistics are victims of an inhibition. Somebody in the past has affirmed that philology is dry and hard. Hearers have repeated the dictum; it has passed from mouth to mouth — yea, from mind to mind — until it now forms a regular item of student vocabulary and (what is more serious) of student belief. Nearly all our beliefs, I fancy, start in this fashion. One person makes a dogmatic statement, either because he has had an exceptional experience, or because he wishes to be thought different, or simply because he can think of nothing else to say. Little by little the notion spreads, like *la calunnia* in the *Barbiere*; little by little it affirms itself; and lo and behold! we have a *credo*, which takes possession of the will of its adherents. At that point, resistance becomes impossible. If you are once absolutely convinced that you cannot do a thing, that thing thereby is made undoable. It is out of the power of a human creature to do a thing which he is sure he cannot do. He is like a hen held with its head planted against a line on the ground, and, when the restraining hand is removed, strangely unable to stir. (To this peculiarity of men and hens I shall revert later.) My present point is that a given student, once converted to faith in the impossibility of acquiring "philology," becomes *ipso facto* incapable of acquiring it.

Like or dislike of this or that branch of knowledge is a matter of fashion, even as are the sounds we give to English words. For a large part of my fellow-citizens, the pronunciation *fahst, ahfter, cahn't*, and so on, is a product of over-elegant affectation, to be either rejected with manly scorn or surreptitiously and shamefacedly cultivated. In point of fact, its beginning was quite lowly; it invaded English literary idiom as a vulgarism late in the eighteenth century, and, as far as our country is concerned, gained greatest favor and widest extension among Yankee farmers. Gradually, in a restricted category of words, it then found promotion to the fashionable utterance of Old and New England.

This example offers easy return passage to the point from which we started, to wit, the science of linguistics, which had its birth in the golden cloud of German Romanticism. Yes, that science which youths and maidens now dub prosaic and repellant, was in its inception as poetic as Euphorion, child of Faust and Helen of Troy. An overmastering, fanatical, mystical fondness for the primitive and the popular swept over Europe, as you know, a century since, a dominant factor in the great Romantic movement. At the same time came a triumph of science and a reshaping of scientific method. Of these twain was born Philology, whose poetic origin was long manifest in her works. Both language and literature fell sharply into two camps, the popular and the learned; the favorite in each case, the charmer in letters, the fascinator in speech, was ever the poetry and the idiom conceived as popular. The voice of the people was the voice of God.

Was it not a solemn article of faith that so-called "popular" poetry was an actual collaborative product of the people? Of course we did not really imagine the inhabitants of a country standing in a row, numbering themselves, like recruits — the first shouting *arma*, the second *virumque*, the third *cano*, until they had completed the *Æneid*. No, we did not imagine this, because the *Æneid* is an "art poem." But although, even for "folk productions," like the *Iliad*, the *Nibelungenlied*, and the *Chanson de Roland*, we avoided explicit postulation of such a picture, we did hold fast to a cult which, in its implications, vaguely adumbrated it. The folk, to be sure, did not line itself up in a white heat and create the *chef-d'œuvre* all at once; no, rather did the creative populace, by some mysterious feat of transmission, evolve the naive masterpiece mouth to mouth and generation by generation. This we did believe, firmly. Not yet, indeed, have we quite outlived this pretty parthenogenetic idea. But year by year the distinction between primitive and sophisticated art grows fainter and harder to trace. Is any art ever unconscious? If so, where shall we look for it — at what stage in the development of *homo sapiens* or *desipiens*? All that we can know is that some one composes and others compose after his style. I am ready to admit instinct, or divine inspiration, for number one; but for the following numbers we must invoke an additional motive, the most active, incessant, and fruitful of all human impulses: imitation.

As in poetry, so in speech. The medium of nearly all our communication, poetic or otherwise, is language; and language is perpetually changing. Why, we know not; yet change it does, more rapidly at some stages than at others, but never stopping. Furthermore, when we assemble, as best we may, the vocabulary of a language and tabulate its transformations from age to age, we detect, for each people and period, an amazing congruity. If Old

English *hūs* becomes modern *house*, *mūs* will turn up as *mouse*, and we may expect *cū* to develop into cow, *mūth* into *mouth*. So, in French, we find Latin *carum* giving *cher*, *canem* becoming *chien*, *cantum* turning to *chant*, and, if we were over hasty, we should infer that Latin *c* at the beginning of a word always is transformed to French *ch*; but when we observe *centum* and *cent*, *civitatem* and *cité*, we are obliged to restrict our rule, and, after examining different environments, to confine it to *c* before *a*. Thus, by comparing various sets of words, we arrive at certain fixed principles which the language has followed in its evolution. In speech, however, as in literature, one is led to make a distinction between popular and bookish words, the latter, late introductions into the oral stock, having been subject to fewer transforming influences. This distinction, while not so simple as it once seemed, has maintained itself better than the similar classification of poetry. For instance, while *caput* in popular parlance has become *chef*, erudite *capitalem* remains *capital*; so one and the same word, *captivum*, as an old-time everyday term becomes *chétif*, but as a bookish borrowing retains an almost Latin form, *captif*.

Here are strange phenomena. Little wonder it is that the mysterious consistencies running through the popular element of human speech should have impressed Romantic grammarians as due to natural laws, similar to the laws which determine the orbits of the planets or which govern the speed of falling bodies. "Sound laws" the Romantics called them, or "phonetic laws." Now a natural law, as distinguished from a man-made one, is inviolable. Phonetic laws, then, admit of no exceptions. Speech came to be conceived as something existing by itself, independently of the people who spoke it. At this point the supernatural makes its appearance as a dominant factor in otherwise naturalistic reasoning. For what else than supernatural is a mysterious, inexorable, unerring force which shapes language to its will, regardless of the volition or consciousness of the speakers? As in the Romantic conception of poetry the folk as a whole produced something radically different from the possible product of any individual, so language, an entity beyond control of the community or of its members, pursued a course dictated by an inner law of its own. At a given period, some secret urge impelled all the members of a nation to change every *u* to *ou*, or every *ca* to *cha*, in current speech; when this urge manifested itself, there was no withstanding it. Like grace in Jansenist theology, it was irresistible, and it struck where it listed. Attempts, to be sure, many and painful attempts, were made to ascribe its blind decrees to race, climate, or other condition or circumstance; but they seldom persuaded any but their author. A deep, dark mystery it remained, this Romantic force, whether physical or psychic.

But a law, to be respected, must not suffer too many and too manifest violations. And the further one progressed in the history of language, the more one was obliged to excuse and explain away non-conformities of increasingly numerous types, to balance one law against another which did not run parallel to it, to attribute an ever growing proportion of phenomena to analogy, which is another name for imitation. Just as a new hat worn by a social leader may determine the shape of hats in a whole neighborhood; and the neighborhood, if a prosperous and pushing one, may transform the headgear of a town; and the town may conceivably alter the hat-fashion of an entire country: so one mode of inflection in one verb may incline to its pattern other and originally dissimilar verbs and ultimately establish in the language a new conjugation. This power of analogy was of course recognized from the start; but one rather tried to keep it in the background, and to limit to the utmost of one's ingenuity the number of derelicts for which its S.O.S. call was used. In our day infractions of phonetic law have, nevertheless, so pushed to the fore as almost to obscure the law itself.

Most of the older conceptions of language were tacitly based, more or less, on the idea that linguistic transformations either had stopped some time ago, like the evolution of species, or were now carried on in a fashion fundamentally different from the good old law-abiding style of yore. In fact, when we consider the speech that environs us in one country, in one state, in one town, even in one street, we find the very negation of consistency. I am not consistent with myself; and I venture to guess that not one of you can be taken as a safe example of the inviolability of sound-laws. It is only in large masses, and in considerable epochs, that the principles emerge clearly; and even under those conditions phenomena are sadly mixed by migration. Once, after giving careful and eager ear to the dialect of an old lady whom I met in Wales, I discovered, in parting, that she came from Scotland. Really, remembering the disturbing elements, one is amazed, not at the degree of nonconformity but at the existence of any conformity at all.

But conformity there is, for each more or less isolated community, in every considerable lapse of time, for certain large classes of words which form, so to speak, the backbone of its vocabulary. However we may smile at the Romantic conception of a mysterious racial urge, the mystery still remains, as mysterious and baffling as ever. We are now aware that sound-changes, like changes in conjugation or declension, may be highly contagious, that an infection in one word may spread, either slowly or rapidly, to other words of similar type, just as one rotten apple in a barrel may bring decay to all its companions. If, for instance, people for some reason began saying *dahnce* for *dance*, it would be natural enough for *France, lance, prance* to fall into line; and over-zealous Americans might even say *fahncy* for *fancy*, under a mistaken impression that they were acquiring a British accent. Some of our gradations of vowels may, in fact, have come about in this way, although even then the reason for the alteration in the pioneer word must still remain a mystery. In most categories, however, such evidence as we possess seems to indicate that whole groups of words shifted their sounds together: that *mūs* and *hūs* and *cū*, for example, developed an *ow* from their *u*, not successively, but simultaneously or nearly so; that *caput* and *canem* and *cantum* were contemporaries in the alteration of their *c* into *ch*. "Seems to indicate" is the most we can say, obliged as we are to study our phenomena in long historical periods and in texts of mixed provenience.

Let us look at the question from another point of view. How do such transformations take place within the limits of our own personal experience? We have all had occasion to witness some peaceful revolutions. It is not long since people began saying *citee, prettee* for *city* and *pretty*, a fashion that has spread rapidly through large regions of the United States and Australia. I can distinctly remember when I first heard *cud, wud, shud, gud* for

could, would, should, good. At first it shocked and
disgusted me; but ere long, to my horror, I would
find myself just on the brink of falling into the
practice. In point of fact, the evolutionary steps
which we are privileged to witness do not, like in-
fluenza, affect a whole community at once, but
spread, like measles, from person to person. A
popular preacher for some reason mispronounces a
common word; his error is repeated by his congre-
gation, and, if they are wealthy people, by other
frequenters of the same social haunts, until the mistake of one decade has become the standard of the
decade after. Let us suppose that a trans-Missis-
sippian speaker, in pursuit of homely vigor, keeps
his lips apart when he pronounces, by way of enthusiastic approval, the word *good.* His hearers,
impressed by the forcefulness of this unaccustomed
exclamation, make it their own; and, having once
acquired *gud,* naturally accompany it with *cud,*
shud, wud; until at last, in their usage, every short
oo is shorn of the protecting cover of the lips, and
we have *stud* for *stood,* then *fut* for *foot, luck* for
look, and so on. The new vogue thus locally established widens its area month by month; within the
year Massachusetts will be following Texas.

Thus, to the best of my belief, are most evolu-
tions of language to be accounted for. We start
with a deviation from the norm, such as in scientific
parlance we term a "sport." The sport may be at

the origin confined to a single word and an individual speaker; or it may appear simultaneously in several words or in several persons. We may be able to guess at a cause, or we may not. It is like mutation in a plant. At any rate, the sport, once in existence, diffuses itself by means of imitativeness, the great primal instinct of humanity. To begin with, a small abnormality; then imitation, to preserve it and propagate it. Who knows how far such a theory may be carried in explanation of all phases of evolution? I confine myself to the one strictly human phase: speech. For speech, in the physical world, is the one attribute which all men possess and which is possessed by man alone.

I have called imitativeness "the great primal instinct of humanity." But this instinct, though universal in man, is not peculiar to our race. Other creatures possess it in abundant measure, particularly those animals which are generally regarded as more or less akin to our own remote ancestors. Indeed, our ample heritage of imitative proclivity might be cited as apparent evidence of our simian descent. Should we rehearse in detail all the acts which we perform in the course of a day, from waking up in the morning to going to bed at night, how many of them could you trace to any other source than communal habit? Nearly all the acts of our lives are done simply because other people do them. Sometimes we are conscious of our sub-

servience, oftener we are not. This last statement
may be made also with specific reference to speech,
our greatest common activity and our most precious common possession. When the child first tries
to shape words as he hears them, how far is he
aware of what he is doing? When the boy adopts
a new slang phrase current in school, what element
of purpose is there in his act of conformity? When
you first began to say *att all* for *at-all*, to what extent were you conscious of an effort? I am inclined,
from my own observation, to give a high rating to
the conscious as compared with the involuntary.
And so, in the whole evolution of language, I am
inclined to give to desire and purpose a much more
important function than has generally been accorded them. More and more skeptically do I
listen to discussion of primitive language and popular speech. Savages who possess no clothes and no
alphabet possess professional rhetoricians whose
studied utterances are an amazement and a model
to their hearers; so I have been told by the son of
an African chief. The tough jargon of the East
Side of New York is, I fancy, as meticulously acquired and as proudly exhibited as the daintiest
eloquence of the mellifluous highbrow. Have you
never watched a baby face, in profound contemplation of the possibilities of a new word?

Inborn, surely, is the gift of copying; but it is
also the most assiduously cultivated of our gifts.

We speak of cultivating originality, of developing self-expression. What we really cultivate is imitation; what we express is not ourselves, but somebody else — although, if we are ostentatiously eccentric, we may express it by negation. When you declare: "it is sweet and beautiful to die for one's country," what you mean is, "people say and believe it is sweet and beautiful to die for one's country"; but if you cynically assert: "it is not sweet and beautiful to die for one's country," you are stating the same thing. Squirm and squeal as we may, we cannot escape servitude. We are the slaves of everyone else, and most of us enjoy the bondage. And why not? Is not imitation the clearest proof of the brotherhood of man; and what is more comforting than the consciousness of that solidarity? Brothers we are and brothers we shall always be, from the first monkey to the last man. How language originated, nobody knows and everybody has told. We are all tired of discussing the subject, but we all continue to do so. Is there any more fascinating problem, or any more completely elusive? We do not know at what stage of evolution speech set in, whether the sounds made by the so-called lower animals constitute speech, nor can we be sure, in fact, what speech is. Anthropologists have told us the bits of skull left us by prehistoric types of man indicate that the speech-making part of the brain existed in the earliest

models. But do they really know? My confidence
has never been the same since the discovery, a few
years ago, of a human tooth in strata of the American plains so deep as to indicate a form of man as
primitive as the denizens of Heidelberg or Nean-
derthal. Indeed, from this small specimen, it was
possible to reconstruct the whole person, and enter-
prising journals published his (or her) portrait, no
doubt as good a likeness as many newspaper pictures. And then it suddenly came out that the
tooth in question had belonged, not to a man, but
to a peccary, a beast long extinct — and therefore
interesting — in North America. My acquaintance
with the animal being limited to the information
afforded by the *Swiss Family Robinson*, I cannot
say how nearly identical with our own is the dentition of the peccary. At any rate, it deceived the
experts. "Beware of the expert" was the theme of
a homily I once heard from Mr. Andrew Carnegie.
"Listen to all the specialists have to tell you, and
then decide for yourself," was his doctrine; "the
specialist is by vocation incapable of seeing more
than one side." I suppose I should have better ap-
preciated his discourse at the time, had I not been
one of the experts involved. Carnegie's principle
applies, I dare say, to specialists in all fields. I
recall the one and only agreement ever reached, to
my knowledge, by economists the world over; it
was reached in the early months of 1914 and was

to the effect that no great war could nowadays endure more than two weeks.

The purpose of this digression is to rehabilitate the layman. After all, his conjecture is not of necessity one of those which for charity's sake had best be quietly overlooked. In the great field of the unknown, anyone's guess may chance to hit the mark, and the unknown is all around us and within us. There are considerable portions of the brain (so I am told by the most eminent brain-surgeon I have met) whose functions, if they have any, are a complete mystery; they are the so-called "uncharted areas"; one may cut out of these districts considerable helpings without perceptible detriment to the mental or physical processes of the patient. Even admitting, however, that the brain-quarter addicted to the fabrication of speech is really present in the oldest human cranium unearthed, does it follow that the wearer of that cranium spoke? Did speaking develop the bump, or did the bump make speaking possible? Again the old problem of the hen and the egg. My own notion is that speech is a distinctly human invention — the one invention which put a great gulf between him and the other beasts. However and whenever he hit upon this all-important device, the first inventor must have been imitated with all possible celerity by fellow-creatures, while the other animals, if they tried to imitate him, failed miserably. Only a few fowls have succeeded in making his sounds, and they apparently have not had the understanding to use them. For utterance in itself is of no avail; there must be an established connection between a sound-group and a concept of some kind. The secret lies in the primal establishment of this relation, and to this secret we have no clue. Was it for a while an esoteric cult; were the first speakers wizards? Likely enough. I am told that in India the composition of music, or of the higher type of music, is an attribute of the priesthood, jealously reserved and transmitted by them, the notes never being written. Thus it may have been with language. Jespersen has expressed the opinion that man sang before he spoke. Music and language may well have been conserved together.

When speech did get out of bondage, either by an escape of the esoteric practice or through invention of a new one, it must have spread like fire. Fire is a good analogy; for fire, too, must, it would seem, have betrayed its utility by accident, and it must have been kept alive by a priesthood, before men discovered the means of making it. Eventually it became the possession of virtually all mankind. So we may imagine how the fitness of sounds to designate things may have come accidentally to man's consciousness, and how it was cultivated, first by the elect, then by the general. A prime factor in its spread was of course the human proneness to imitation. Can we gain any notion of its propagation from the speed with which a baby of today learns to speak? A child left with almost no companionship until the age of two, and therefore virtually speechless up to that time, will in four or five months acquire a considerable vocabulary and the ability to form very simple sentences. I suspect its pronunciation is better than it would have been had its mother been plying it, from the outset, with baby-talk; for I am sure the greater part of the phonetic inaccuracy of infantile prattle is due, not to incorrect, but to correct, imitation — that is, to meticulous copying of the style of its doting elders. But had the pithecanthropic baby the mimetic faculty of our own offspring? That we cannot tell. Monkeys, while marvelously apt in reflecting human acts, show no aptitude in reproducing human sounds, although in company they keep up a deafening chatter of their own. Probably this gibberish answers all their simian needs, and their contact with *homo sapiens* excites visual but not auditive stimuli to emulation. It may be that, like some of our fellows, they talk too much to listen; an over-garrulous person, you have probably observed, seldom learns a foreign language well, because he hears only himself for nine-tenths of the time.

The relation of thought to speech is another puzzle. Can we actually reason without words? I do not believe we can. Certain intuitions, certain reactions may be mute, but genuine argument demands formulation, vocal, visual, or mental. Doubtless it was not always thus. Other creatures, destitute of language, are surely capable of reason to a very limited extent, sufficient for their primitive wants. Dogs and horses, to be sure, from their constant association with our kind, seem to have carried rational processes further than the less fortunate creatures that have not enjoyed the privilege of our companionship. Their requirements have become more complex, more artificial, and a corresponding degree of mental artistry seems to have ensued. I fancy our ancestors, when they first reached the human stage, made shift to reason, as far as necessity demanded, without a vocabulary. But as soon as vocables came into their possession, ratiocination snatched at the opportunity they afforded for clearness and abundance. Little by little, I believe, man formed the habit of reasoning with words until he lost the power of reasoning without them. As Jean-Jacques Rousseau observed (and he never said anything truer), the luxury of one generation becomes the necessity of the next. When we, either as a race or as individuals, have learned to walk on our hind legs, it becomes impossible to proceed comfortably or profitably on all fours. Here again is a habit, the habit of erect or semi-erect posture, doubtless ini-

Pierce Library
Eastern Oregon University
1410 L Avenue
La Grande, OR 97850

tiated by the venturesome few and unthinkingly copied by the *polloi*.

Did our remote ancestors dwell in trees or on the ground? Here is another question on which experts disagree. Even the adoption of a hind-legged gait points to analogies in both directions. Birds, which are largely arboreal, have developed a front-legged locomotion for their tree-life, a hind-legged one for terrestrial progression. A few big ones, however, which have abandoned the tree altogether, have lost the use of their wings. As to their very remote kin, lizards and the like, at home both aloft and on deck, they have decided to be quadrupedal. Sundry monstrous and ungainly reptiles, now happily extinct, seem to have wandered over the ground somewhat after the fashion of the kangaroo, now hopping on their rear feet, now hitching along on both pairs. Snakes, like whales and porpoises, having habituated themselves to a gliding or slipping movement over earth or through water, have discarded, or nearly discarded, all their limbs. Tree-climbing fishes, I believe, have strongly accentuated their anterior extremities; but so have seals, which in a state of nature do not climb trees. Coming down to our kind, we find that monkeys, our distant four-footed cousins, dwell mostly in the foliage, while the apes, which most nearly resemble us, occasionally adopt an upright carriage for impressiveness, if not for horizontal advance. The new-born human babe has a hand-grip suggestive of an arboreal clutch, it has prehensile toes, it has the remnants of a tail, and its first mode of self-displacement is a crawl; yet it is not long satisfied with the crouching posture, and, despite all manner of humiliating and painful experiences, persists in its efforts until it has permanently renounced, for walking, the use of its hands. Query: would the infant have manifested the urge to walk if it had not seen adults walking? Answer: it probably would, though perhaps not so early. The craving to rise to the feet is inborn; it is earlier than man. In many respects, doubtless in this, the development of the individual child epitomizes the history of the race. Innate, too, is the desire to make a noise. But the impulse to utilize noise as a systematic means of communication belongs, as far as we know, not to the mysterious category which we call by the self-protective name "instinctive"; it is a fruit of discovery and imitation.

The problem which in the foregoing inconclusive paragraph I have been trying to approach is this: did men learn to talk while sitting in trees, like parrots, or promenading under them, like Adam and Eve? Have we any indication whatever? In the child, the desire to talk and the desire to walk appear almost simultaneously, although in both respects there is a very considerable variation between one child and another. If we are to carry out the analogy between the individual and the race, we may surmise that *homo*, whether *sapiens* or *insipiens*, began his first speech-exercises at about the period when he started his two-legged daily dozen. Yet we must remember that the cautious adverb (or preposition) "about" may cover a deviation of thousands of years. However, inasmuch as physical evolution is normally slow, and imitation is fast, let us assume that the experimental period of walking included the prentice stage of speech; that the Heidelberg man, for instance, though not yet quite straight on his pins, had gone beyond lesson one in his language course.

Are there in language itself any proofs of early or late acquisition, of arboreal or terrestrial habitat? Experts in comparative philology have deduced from parallel columns of the various Aryan vocabularies a certain common stock which throws a dim light on primitive Aryan civilization. A very dim light, to be sure, because etymologies and affinities, in that crepuscular country, are so uncertain. One has tried to work out similar inferences for the Germanic family; even for the Romance, which is of so recent date as to make the quest almost superfluous. In the general field of comparative philology, the Romance territory is the least obscure, because students have at their disposal both ends of the development; the source, Latin, is

known at least approximately, while the ultimate
outcome — the neo-Latin group — is under our
eyes. The further we go back, of course, the more
nebulous and hypothetical the business becomes.
For Indo-European we have at our disposal neither
any account of the beginning nor any accurate
record of the end. The pursuit of so ghost-like a
science requires not only exceptional acumen, but
also constant and strenuous endeavor to keep in
contact with reality; else the reconstruction of a
vanished speech will become a work of visual
imagination, an accumulation of unpronounceable
combinations of letters and unthinkable combinations of words. Only close observation of the actual
behavior of speech will afford a sane control for the
investigation of its prehistoric conduct. We have
happily rid ourselves of the notion that our great-
grandfathers on "the highlands of Asia" (wherever
that may be) discoursed in roots; for we have
learned that an etymological root is only a scientific
abstraction, a greatest common divisor, so to speak,
of a family of words evidently related. Not yet,
however, are we quite emancipated from the idea
that a branch of the human race at one time talked
straight "Indo-European," or "Indo-Germanic,"
or "Aryan," as one chooses to call it, forgetting
that our assumed Indo-European language is just as
truly a scientific abstraction as the "root" which
was once thought to be its standard unit.

Still more cautious must we be when we speculate about the very birth of speech. Not that we must refrain from all speculation. That is too much to expect, for it is the nature of man to guess, and, besides, all knowledge is more or less speculative; but we must recognize our guesses as guesses and not try to impose them as fact on other sportsmen whose expectation is that a different horse will win. That is the beginning and the end of tolerance — and, I may add, of real science. Now, when one contemplates the combined vocabulary of mankind, as far as one knows anything about it, one fails to detect any distinct arboreal, terrestrial, or maritime flavor. The same thing, I fancy, may be said of human superstitions, taken as a whole. Human conduct, taken as a whole, is, to be sure, plainly terrestrial rather than arboreal or maritime; but that fact simply marks *homo*'s ancestry as a land-race from the time when the waters were divided from the earth, and as a plodding rather than a climbing race either before or after the invention of speech. No, for my part, I can discern agreement in only two principles of communication: first, all men have chosen for their intercourse audible rather than visual signs; second, all men have chosen to produce those audible signs by means of the respiratory organs. With regard to the first election, it is obvious that the choice was limited: sight and hearing are the only ones among our senses that offer a considerable variety; and we have no reason to suppose that man ever had more senses than he has now. One suspects others in other creatures. Birds and many insects seem to have a sense of direction which we lack; and by insects I do not mean our ordinary ants, which are wofully deficient in it. If you doubt our lack, try to find your way in the dark, or in a thick fog, with no sound to guide you. Moreover, some beasts and perhaps most birds appear to possess a means of conveying information which we cannot divine. If a solitary sea-gull finds food, in a spot remote from its kind, presently a swarm of gulls will appear from all quarters apparently condensing from the air. But man, as far as we can judge, has always had the same senses, although their number varies greatly according to the school of psychology to which one belongs. And, although his sense of smell may once have been very much acuter, even rivaling, perhaps, that of the dog, smell is at best a passive sense, so to speak, in that its possessor cannot produce the varieties it registers. The same thing is normally true of touch, however abnormally helpful it may be to the blind. There remain sight and hearing. The active partner of sight is the whole power of motion; the active partner of audition is the whole power of making noise.

Between these two partnerships all mankind has chosen, and all mankind has made the same elec-

tion. One can guess why. The resources of sound
are virtually infinite; those of motion, though
great, are restricted. Sign languages, ingeniously
developed by savage tribes, can tell only a limited
list of things; and I am inclined to suspect that,
such as they are, they presuppose for their development the existence of some sort of spoken medium.
Sign language is to sound language as picture-
writing is to print. Visual symbols, however,
though universally rejected as a principal means,
have remained as a highly useful auxiliary, in the
form of gesture and facial expression. Furthermore, we must not forget that, ever since the invention of spelling, it has been possible to convey the
spoken word to the eye. At present, indeed, there
is a prospect that the eye-symbol may detach itself
from the ear-symbol which it was meant to represent; that the shadow may break away from the
body that casts it, and try to lead a separate existence; in other words, that our language, and all
other languages as stupidly misspelled (if there be
any such) may break into two, one for the eye and
one for the ear. One result would be that the unfortunate schoolboy would have two mother tongues
to learn; another would be that the reader or
writer would no longer hear mentally what he reads
or writes and consequently would lose all sense of
rime, rhythm, and style. And the educational experts are doing their best to precipitate such a

catastrophe by their advocacy of "eye reading" or "silent reading."

Sound, then, has been preferred to motion by all the races of men. Not only that: the races have all chosen the same method of producing sound. This unanimity does not signify so much, however, for there is only one effective way, as far as man is concerned. Insects, to be sure, can make themselves stridently heard by rubbing their thighs against their bellies, but we have no such facility. Crustaceans, fishes, and reptiles seem to be virtually voiceless. We men, if we wish, can make a noise by clapping our hands; but it is only one noise — and that one is in fact sometimes used for speech purposes, to express approbation or command. There would appear to be nothing left; and therefore men, beasts, and birds concur in the use of the respiratory apparatus, which is a wind instrument in continuous potential operation. I mean that the lungs supply a constant stream of air running in and out through the windpipe, with intake and outlet through the mouth and nose, and with the possibility of endless variation by shifts of intervening organs — glottis, false glottis, epiglottis, pharynx, velum, arches, tongue, jaw, and lips. Now, it so happens that nature, usually so extravagant, has once in a while an impulse of economy and uses an organ for a double purpose. This is notably the case with the breathing machine, a part of which is utilized for the internalizing of food. In fact all the organs just enumerated, above the windpipe, have to do with the absorption of nourishment: lips, jaw, tongue, arches, velum, pharynx, epiglottis have to do with taking it in and forwarding it on its way to the stomach; while epiglottis, false glottis, and glottis keep triple guard over the windpipe, excluding therefrom any particle addressed to the stomach *via* the aesophagus; for misdelivery would cause painful, even fatal, consequences. A highly developed mechanism results, and this intricately delicate machinery happens to be exactly what is needed for the production of speech. I say "happens" in order to avoid an unscientifically religious or teleological implication.

Even so, there is still a possibility of choice, for the air runs both in and out. But here the selection is, as the French say, "indicated" by our degree of control — unless, indeed, that difference in control is itself the result of our loquacious habit. At any rate, the intake, or inspiration, is comparatively short and fairly uniform, while the outflow, or expiration, can, within reasonable limits, be regulated at will. Thus all men, under normal conditions, use for utterance the outflowing stream of breath. But the inflow has its occasional expressive functions, too, as when, for instance, a gasp of surprise or pain is called for. In fact, mankind, taken as a whole, in its development of speech wastes very few possibilities, although the different peoples of our race differ considerably in their notion of waste and economy. As far as I can see, the only chances universally neglected are the whistle, the sneeze, and the snore; and even the latter, in a highly mitigated form, serves as a type of *r* — the "uvular *r*," as it is called, or, more popularly and less exactly, the "guttural *r*." If the sneeze is scorned, the cough is not; for the latter, greatly softened, is the "glottal stop," that unwritten consonant which gives the jarring effect to Danish and which in German precedes every stressed initial vowel. Even the whistle functions as a signal or as a mark of disapproval. The various "clucks," or suction stops, made without the help of the aerial stream, are regular elements of speech in some regions, notably in South Africa. Some of them we Indo-Europeans employ, not as consonants, but as independent interjections: such are the *k*-like "cluck," which starts a horse; the *t*-like one, which denotes reproof; the *p*-like one which betokens intimate affection, and is known as a kiss.

Beasts and birds, too, have a vocal apparatus; the latter, in fact, with their double larynx, would seem to have a certain advantage over humanity. Birds, however, have no lips, and beasts make sparing use of them. I fancy, moreover, that all these creatures have a less intricate respiratory apparatus than man, although the elaboration of it in our species may be due in part to special use. Again the problem of hen and egg. Did man develop speech because his machine was better, or is his machine better because he developed speech? If the latter is true, a reasonable deduction would seem to be that speech came early in his career. I believe, anyhow, that the invention of language is more a matter of wit (and perhaps necessity) than of physical endowment. I believe most creatures have adequate means of producing a speech, if only they had the brain to make use of it. Of course, since language is both give and take, both active and passive, we ought to examine the hearing of other creatures; and on this point we have no satisfactory investigation. We know, to be sure, that many creatures hear more than we do; but can they make such fine distinctions? Fine and therefore numerous distinctions — these are the requisites for extended communication by mouth and ear. Before deciding how responsible birds and beasts are for their failure to create a language, we should have to subject them to a series of audition tests. And should the human ear turn out to be distinctly superior, we should still be confronted with the problem whether this superiority is the cause or the result of our talking habit.

It is generally assumed that man is the latest product of evolution among animate species. It is generally assumed also that man is the best, and that his superiority is due to a bigger, better, and busier brain. His only rival for the domination of the earth is the insect; and the outcome of the contest is still uncertain. The one competitor is strong in mentality, the other in productivity. The latest and the earliest of things that live and move on earth are in the fight for the finish. Each species, as it arose, developed, it would seem, as far as it could go, and then stopped. Man, created on the last working day, was wound up for a higher flight; and, by his invention of speech, followed by that of fire and, much later, by that of writing, he eventually secured control of the elements and the power of maintaining and continuously extending thought and knowledge from generation to generation. Other creatures apparently know only what their remotest ancestors knew; and how these ancestors got their information, God only knows. According to Fabre, the naturalist, God created it in them. Man keeps right on adding to his store, at a breathless rate of acceleration. With speech and writing, he has increased *ad infinitum* the capacity for imitation. All progress is due to a very small number of superior individuals, whose achievement is imitated by the herd; and writing enables us to imitate not only the present, but the past; and in that past, to select the best. Who knows what mute, inglorious discoverer may have existed

among the ants, whose discovery perished with
him, because he could not tell anybody about it?
"He had no poet, and he died." Being mute, the
ant can imitate only what everybody else has imitated for the last thirty million years.

The upshot of all these more or less fanciful con-
siderations is that man is man because he can talk
and can therefore stimulate and control imitation;
that he probably invented talk toward the close of
his material evolution, at the time when he was
becoming physically fit; that his invention does
not reveal his habits nor his habitat at the time he
made it. Speaking of habitat, I have never been
able to understand why the experts assume without
question the unity of man — that is, the doctrine
that he evolved in one Garden of Eden, and not in
several. Perhaps they have reasons of their own,
which are hid away from the layman. As to the
location of that Eden, they disagree, from pole to
equator. Was it in Java, in South Africa, in central
Europe, in England? For aught I care (and aught
I know), language may have been invented independently in all these localities, the inventors being
possessed of essentially the same physical equip-
ment and the same urge to imitation. It may even
have been born and died, again and again, as races
developed and disappeared; the important fact is,
it survived with the surviving race and is per-
petuated in ourselves.

Speech has survived in the human race, but it has assumed countless different forms. If we were striving for perfect accuracy, we might set up the principle, *quot homines tot linguae*; but when we came to apply it, we should find that it was both too broad and too restricted. For not only has every man at different stages of his life different modes of speech, but at one and the same stage, if he is a civilized being, he has several styles, according to circumstances and environment. The aquatic vehicle which at home I call a *boat* is in my summer abode nearly a *butt*; I point *northward* to the poet, *no'tha'd* to the seaman; the hoisting apparatus which in talking to you I should designate as a *tackle* becomes in converse with mechanics a *taycle*. *Loam* for the gardener is *loom*. On the other hand, the small differences between individual and individual of the same community do not seriously interfere with intelligibility; otherwise, either these unevennesses would be leveled out or two distinct dialects would be started, and the latter result, under present conditions of quick communication, is virtually impossible in our type of civilization. Imitation maintains in speech the power to fulfil its double purpose, which is to tell and to understand. Why, then, has language ever been differentiated? The answer is obvious: because in earlier phases of culture mankind was split into little groups, each in its own valley or its own island, and these groups, each in itself homogeneous, had little need of communicating with one another and little facility for doing so. If, when speech was first invented, the steamship, the railway, the automobile, the airship, the telegraph, the telephone, the radio, and the radio-announcer had been in operation, there would have been no Tower of Babel.

At this point, however, another question arises. Since intercourse, in primitive days, was scanty between village and village, how comes it that in very large stretches of territory the village dialects, while unmistakably distinct from one another, show a marked resemblance, as compared with the dialects of other large stretches? Why are there languages as well as local dialects? Here the answer must be multiple, for various causes have operated. In the first place, while, at the dawn of civilization, village is cut off from village, the isolation is not complete; one hamlet fights with another or trades with another, and for that reason each imitates its neighbor sufficiently to preserve or to create understanding.

Then we have the phenomenon of migration, many communities combining on the march, amalgamating, carrying into strange lands a partially unified type of speech, which then spreads out in fresh pastures, settles in new valleys, and begins once more to differentiate, while keeping always a reminder of its common origin. Often, to be sure, the speech of the immigrants mixes more or less with that of the earlier inhabitants, as happened more than once in England; sometimes one swallows up the other — that is, the newcomers imitate the old settlers, as the Germanic tribes did when they moved over into the Roman Empire; or the old stagers copy the dominant intruders, as the Celts did when overrun by conquering Latins; sometimes two languages maintain themselves for centuries side by side, with comparatively little mixture, as English and French in Canada, English and Indian in the United States, English and German in Pennsylvania and our Middle West. It is all a question of whether imitation is worth while. Suppose a new family, of different social status, moves into your street; in the natural course of things, if that family is richer and better connected than you, you will begin to copy its ways; if it is poorer and humbler, it will try to mimic you; if there is a possible difference of opinion with regard to respective social eminence, both parties will bristle with independence; if proximity brings no contact, new and old will pursue their old habits undisturbed.

Political union forms the last stage (perhaps I should say "latest," not "last," for I cannot read the future). In a broad stretch of land one district becomes dominant, imposing its control upon others, until there emerges a country, with a capital; and the dialect of the capital is imitated by the provincials, whose local idioms it may eventually supersede entirely. Thus it has happened, or is happening, in France, in England, in Spain. In Italy, the dominating force has been cultural rather than political or military, and the obscuration of local dialects has not progressed so far.

We find, then, on our globe, a variety of languages, as we find a variety of races; but races and languages do not always match; the distribution is not identical, for peoples have borrowed to and fro. Indeed, it is impossible to say just what a race is; there are no sure and generally accepted criteria. We all know that there are several distinct types of mankind, but exactly how they differ, where one stops and another begins, nobody can tell, not even the expertest expert. This being the case, there is little prospect of answering the frequent question whether fundamental differences in speech are due to racial differences in physique. As far as our experience goes, the answer is negative. A French child, a Chinese child, even an African child, brought up from infancy in England and isolated from contact with its parent stock, will speak English exactly like an Englishman. At least, that is my impression; I wonder whether you all agree. The thick lips of the African incline him to substitute a labial for a labiodental, — to say, for instance, *lub* for *love*, — but they do not make such substitution necessary. I suspect that a rapid, even respiration lies behind the swift utterance of the Japanese and their lack of tonic accent; but the mode of breathing is doubtless a habit rather than a consequence of structure. Presumably the employment of clucks as speech elements and the systematic use of pitch as a language factor may be attributed in some fashion to habits, but one does not see how. Certain qualities of voice we associate with certain languages, — one quality with the Negro, another with the Chinese, — yet the connection is by no means universal; doubtless it, too, is a matter of habit. Has the strange development of throat-sounds in Arabic anything to do with the sands of the desert?

As one reflects on such puzzles, one is moved once more to inquire whether influence may not operate both ways, whether structure may not be affected by linguistic habit. We are familiar with the result of use and disuse of organs in the general scheme of evolution; we have in our own experience evidence of the effect of exercise on the development of muscle — compare the swelling biceps of the athlete with the flabby or withered arm of the inactive. To such an inert member would I liken the velum and the lips of a large proportion of my fellow-countrymen in the Middle West, who appear to me to be suffering from partial atrophy of those organs. Inertia of the lips while they speak is immediately evident to the eye, for their mouth-slit, never really open, seldom alters its shape. Atrophy of the velum, or soft palate, together with a curious constriction of the pharynx, reveals itself to the ear in a constant dull nasality. Are these phenomena matters of habit or of muscular decline? Originally, no doubt, they were habits carried west from New England, which probably derived them from Puritan Old England. With regard to the lips I am not sure; perhaps they might be stirred to activity by volition, although unconscious imitation seems not to suffice. But in the case of the pharynx and velum I am almost convinced that actual deterioration has set in, since I find that rhetoricians and even some expert phoneticians are unable to correct the intense nasality which they surely must recognize as a blemish (and which, by the way, prevents a good utterance of the French nasals).

One need not assume, however, that all nose-talkers are victims of physical degeneracy. For a nasal twang, like stuttering, provokes imitation; its lure, indeed, is well-nigh irresistible. Its origin, as far as our language is concerned, is, I think, to be found in religion. There seems to be an inherent connection between sanctimoniousness and nasality. One hears the nose-note in divine service even in Catholic churches in sunny climes; it enhances, to be sure, the audibility of the voice, but I greatly doubt whether this is its *raison d'être*. At any rate, while a moderate nasal resonance may be a desideratum in singing, the full blast of the *fossæ*, as used in the French nasals, is found by French singing-teachers to be a nuisance, as it makes the vowels sound out of tune. Whatever the cause, nasality, it would seem, was an attribute of righteousness among the English Puritans, who carried it with them to our shores. After coloring New England speech for many generations, perhaps fostered by a climate inimical to the wide-open mouth, it followed the western trail into the great central plain, where it lingers, as I said. Meanwhile in New England it has been dying out — and not alone, I believe, because of the decay of piety. That has been one source of the decline, no doubt; but another factor has been imitation of non-nasal Europeans, with whom Yankeeland is in continual touch.

Why have parrots so strong a suggestion of nasal twang? It cannot reasonably be attributed to the Puritans, for I am sure those worthy people have never been the parrots' chief preceptors. One is rather driven to the conclusion that the quality in question is due, not to copying, but to inexorable physical necessity: I mean, of course, the beak. We observe, even among human speakers, that a large Roman or hooked nose, with its cavernous pipes, makes its influence perceptible. One would dearly like to know just how the parrot makes its deservedly famous imitations. It has a large, flexible tongue that looks much like ours, and it has apparently a considerable resonator; but, aside from that, I know nothing of its resources. For instance, I cannot conceive how it can shape all the consonants; some of them must be left to our imagination: *k* and *g* it should be able to handle after a fashion, and perhaps *t* and *d*; but how in the world can it tackle *p* or *b* or *m*? Perhaps, as a ventriloquist does, with the tip of the tongue. I have told elsewhere how I once investigated the vocal processes of a duck. It is a comparatively simple matter, because a duck's ordinary conversation is limited to a syllable which we imperfectly imitate as "quack." The vowel in the middle is indeed not unlike our "short *a*," and is made in similar fashion, with beak pretty wide open and tongue in a position that may with some latitude be called "low-front." But neither before nor after the vowel is there any visible occlusion of the passage. The effect of stoppage must be produced in the throat, presumably by closure of the glottis. It is a thing quite within the scope of human imitation. I fancy the "caw" of the crow lends itself to similar analysis. A harder problem is the interpretation of the cat's "meow," which the Italians, by the way, spell *gnau* (or "neow"). The chief difficulty

lies in securing the right observation-point for so
small an area. If one could only magnify the
sounding apparatus five times! That amplification,
together with a favorable inlook, I once obtained
with the help of a mountain lion, which I heard
"meowing" like a cat. I hasten to add that the
mountain lion was in a cage, and I was on the
ground without. First the beast would open wide
its huge mouth with the middle of the tongue
arched up in about the shape of a palatal *n*; then
it would slowly lower the bunched member until a
sonorous *ah* ensued; the final *oo* it produced by
gradually closing its face. Before pursuing these
studies, it was possible for me to give a passable
imitation of the duck, the crow, and the cat by
blind imitation, although I fancy my mimicry
would have excited the derision of the originals,
had they recognized it. But after the above-
described phonetic research I succeeded in producing copies which never could have brought a smile
to the face of the most exacting fowl or beast.
That is the value of a scientific method: it makes
you sure of your results.

Beasts and fowls, though far inferior to man in
their phonetic range, can produce a considerable
variety of sounds; some creatures, indeed, have a
rich repertory. Why? Is the output at their disposal devoted exclusively to self-expression, or can
it be made to serve as a means of communication?

In other words, have the "lower animals" a language? Expert opinions differ, and the inexpert differ still more, their difference bearing on the meaning of the word "language," and on the interpretation of the sundry barks, yowls, grunts, whines, yelps, shrieks, and squawks with which the animal world regales us. I have often listened to them, myself, with growing sympathy, and I have read treatises by men whose observation was far more extensive and sympathetic than mine; but I have failed to discover evidence of anything I should call a language. The utterance of beast and bird seems to me to lack, as far as we can interpret their noises, the two essential elements of language as we conceive it: noun and verb. If it is a speech, it is (I believe) a speech of interjections. It does sometimes serve the purpose of conveying an idea; but I am not sure that the sound in question was intended for that purpose. When a crow lets out a warning note, whereat the whole flock makes off, does the sentry really mean to give the alarm or is he merely voicing his own fear? When a hen gathers in her chicks with an anxious cluck, is she really calling them or is she involuntarily expressing her timorousness? It is all a question of intention. There is no doubt that the crows and the chicks derive something from the "caw" or "cluck"; there is little doubt that these noises have become for the hearers conventional symbols. The question is: have they been so accepted also by the speakers? And that question we may never be able to answer. It may well be that the crows are now just at the stage which we have theoretically assumed as the first step in human speech: recognition of the communicative value of interjections. But we may be sure enough that crows will advance no further. Let us say that we are confronted with a vast assortment of self-expressive interjections, some of which convey a message and may be so intended. Is this language or is it not?

As far as we know, the modes of beast-expression do not develop. The sheep and the frog presumably hold forth today as they held forth in the day of Aristophanes. It must be confessed, though, that we know precious little about it. When one nation interprets the cock's crow as *kikeriki*, another as *cocorico*, another as *cockadoodle-doo*, we cannot attach much importance to any human imitation or description of a beast-cry, ancient or modern. It may be noted, in passing, that all these humanizations of Chanticleer begin with a consonant, whereas the original, to my ear, starts with a vowel, which by its abrupt inception suggests a *k*. Of the three versions, the English is the most fantastic — possibly an indication of the English aptitude for imitation as compared with that of other races. In default, then, of direct evidence for or against our view, we stick to the general theory that the beasts ended their development, including their linguistic achievement such as it may be, ere man had fairly started on his. Possibly, if humanity had advanced earlier, some other creatures, being still at a plastic age, might have imitated us, as the mocking-bird copies other fowls. Parrots, to be sure, and to a small extent ravens and starlings, have accomplished mimicry of us which puts to shame our imitation of them. Whether their success is a sign of tardy evolution on their part, lasting over perhaps into the present or human era, it were futile to conjecture.

Futile also, I fear, is the attempt to dissociate the inherent value of the cry from the conditions under which it is produced. When Sterne's starling says "I can't get out," he is talking English and not starling, and therefore uses a precise term, "out." But let a dog say "I can't get out" and "I can't get in," and I defy anyone to hear a difference; it is the same whine, which on one side of the door means "out," on the other side "in." It is merely a symptom of suppressed desire, of the same stuff his dreams are made on, when he is restless in his sleep. I know a dog of mixed ancestry, who addresses mankind with the deep bay of a hound, and a squirrel with the little shrill bark of I don't know what disreputable parent. He never uses the squirrel-cry to a man, nor the man-cry to a squirrel, doubtless because the emotions (or, to stick to the lingo of the day, the reactions) induced by man and squirrel are quite diverse. When it comes, however, to differentiation of his varied emotions in the presence of man, his vocabulary falls short; an unseeing listener cannot tell "I'm glad to see you" from "get out of here," nor "I'm awfully lonesome" from "what's that noise?" Though varied enough for the expression of a modest gamut of feeling, his outgivings, after all, are very limited, and they are always the same; when one has known him for a week, perhaps even for a day, one never hears anything new. For a growl and a snarl are likely to turn up any day. And his speech is otherwise all vowels; I cannot remember ever having heard a good-natured consonant from a dog, unless we count as such the rather sudden opening of the mouth which we hear sometimes as *b*, sometimes as *w* — "bow-wow," "woof." The *f* at the end of this last word is, I believe, an unvoicing of the vowel, accompanied by a partial closing of the snout.

While the cat does give the impression of something more articulate than the dog, it must be admitted that beast-speech, in general, is a vowel-speech, as contrasted with the utterance of man, strongly diversified and steadied by consonants. The language of animals is essentially a language of interjections in the form mainly of vowels. And, as far as we know, the animal displays freely all that is in him; if he does not give us a greater rich-ness either of sound or of sense, it is presumably because he is physically or mentally incapable of anything more. If, as people used to think, men first got the notion of speech by imitating animals, that notion must have been only a generic one; and, such being the case, there is no need of invok-ing the theory at all, for there is no reason to sup-pose that emotional cries are less instinctive in our kind than in other creatures. We still have a fair number of them, although their place has to some degree been taken by words. "Damn," for in-stance, is not, strictly speaking, a nature-sound, although it does service for several. Actual mim-icry of beast-calls is to be found in the names we give to a few birds, insects, and quadrupeds, such as *cuckoo, bob white, whippoorwill, bow-wow, moo-moo*; and in still fewer nouns and verbs abstracted from them, for example, *peep, hiss, gobble, trill.* Imitation of other noises we may still detect in *bang, shriek, splash, slam, thud, thump*, and their like. The mimetic principle, however, accounts for only an insignificant part of our vocabulary.

Are there, on the other hand, certain suggestions in the very sounds of which words are made? Is there a connection between the abruptness of an explosion, the insinuating persistence of a sibilant, the shrill pitch of an *ee*, the dull tone of *oo*, and some of our fundamental moods? Here we are on

exceedingly slippery ground. There is, to be sure,
a relation between some of the noises we make and
some of the noises nature makes, and this relation,
as we have observed, is utilized in the formation of
a very small number of imitative words. Moreover,
a sharp cluck is manifestly useful for attracting or
checking; a sonorous vowel lends itself to a long-
distance call. Further than this we can hardly go.
One might conceive, *a priori*, that a high-toned
vowel would naturally express *glee*, while a sound
of low pitch would be a fit concomitant of *gloom*;
but, in point of fact, we seldom find examples that
illustrate the theory as conveniently as do the two
words I have chosen. Some people laugh with a
he he! others with a *ho ho!* The interjection *oo!*
may express admiration, enjoyment, or pain. To
the very tempting theory that the motions of the
tongue imitate the impulsive descriptive gestures
of the hands,[1] — one must oppose the dense ignorance of humanity concerning the things it does
within its mouth — not only ignorance, but pre-
posterous misconception, when humanity deigns to
picture these things at all. The contortions of the
face which accompany the first efforts at writing
seem to bear no direct relation to the movements
of the hand. Of somewhat similar nature, based on
the principle of automatic imitation of one part of
the body by another, is the recent theory of an

[1] Sir Richard Paget, *Human Speech.*

Italian scholar that the hand, in creating the characters of script, follows the curves described by the liquid currents in the inner ear under the stimulus of the corresponding sounds.[1] No, human language is built on some other principle. But that principle has been most successful in covering its tracks. All we know is that when Adam named the creatures of earth, Eve repeated the names and taught them to her children. Invention and repetition are the two factors; and the greater of them is repetition.

Nature provided, in our organs of respiration, bounteous opportunities; instinct (whatever instinct may be) supplied the impulse to make noises; human wit perceived, doubtless by accident at first, the possible utility of associating certain noises with certain things, acts, or states. The new idea was fetching, as new fashions are apt to be, and its products, like those of this year's milliner, were copied over and over and over again. As the novel practice developed, it spread, first to your street, then to mine, then to all the streets of the earth, until in the course of ages (for swiftness is a relative thing), man's first and most precious possession, language, stood confessed in all its charm.

This being so, why do we so shy at imitation in the one occupation in which it is the only means of success? I mean, of course, in the study of foreign languages. Why, in this pursuit among all others,

[1] Pietro Tullio, *Das Alphabet*.

do we strive for an originality which elsewhere eludes us? Why, when aiming at French, do we stubbornly stick to Anglo-Saxon self-expression? There are several reasons. First and foremost is the lack of imagination. The same unimaginative temperament which does not allow us, in our own tongue, to think or to talk differently from everybody else, cannot permit us to conceive of a human race which expresses itself in a manner fundamentally different from our own. Necessarily, as we proceed, we become aware of certain tricks of pronunciation and phrasing which are lamentably alien to Main Street, but we judge them to be poor imitations of Main Street usage. If the man of Paris does not talk like the man of Zenith, it is perhaps not his fault, but it is his misfortune. All his peculiarities of accent and of style are due to his failure to copy the real thing. Of course, we never say such rubbish as this; we should probably deny with indignation the existence of such thoughts in our minds. But nevertheless they form the background against which all our practical linguistic efforts are projected. In other words, we suffer from a superiority complex.

The superiority complex, which shows us foreign things, not as they are, but as they appear in comparison with our own perfection, always accompanies a dearth of imagination — is, in fact, one of its commonest manifestations. How in the world, with this spirit dominant within us, shall we ever convince ourselves that the foreigner really knows his own language and is not pitifully trying to ape ours? Convince ourselves we must; that conviction is the first requisite for acquiring any strange tongue. We must actually bring ourselves to believe — and to believe with all our might and all our mind — that the foreigner, however he may fall short in other respects, knows best how to speak and write his native tongue. Having once brought ourselves to this degree of humility, we shall inevitably conclude that our only safety lies in imitation — in abject, servile, unreasoning imitation. A stern conclusion it is, and painful is the practice that it dictates. We must offer up our dignity on the altar of knowledge. We must be willing to make ourselves supremely ridiculous. We have seen how funny the outsider can be when he tries to copy us. Shall we not be equally funny, or even more so, when we attempt to imitate him?

One of the most amusing evidences of our fatuous dullness is our failure to profit by the failures of the outlander when he tries to speak like us. Two students, a German and an American, become close comrades at a German university. Almost daily they plan to meet for exchange of lessons, the German learning to speak English, the American hoping to learn to speak German. Usually one or the other is a bit behind the hour at the appointment. When it is the German, he invariably says: "Excuse me that I am late." The American, with equal persistence, says, — "Entschuldigen Sie mich, spät zu sein." Never does it occur to either that a swap of constructions is as plainly indicated as obliging Fate can ever suggest anything. The Italian, at the close of a polite letter, signs himself "with obsequious greetings, your most devoted"; while his American correspondent, in an effort to avoid the "obsequious," eliminates courtesy with a dry "suo." When the Spaniard wishes to tell you that he has a cold, he declares, "I am constipated," and the unthinking barbarian laughs; but when the barbarian has like information to convey, he phrases it: "He cogido un frio." "I retain two," says the French schoolboy, doing his arithmetic in English; and his translantic schoolmate, after having with difficulty stifled his mirth, responds: "Je porte deux." Always the same fixed idea that ours is the only real way of saying things.

We have here not nationalistic conceit alone, but also the usual failure to distinguish words from thoughts. To the ordinary man in the street, the word *is* the thought, and the thought *is* the word. If you substitute another expression, you are uttering either a different thought or none at all. To translate from one tongue to another, the only safe method, according to George Babbitt, is to render every individual word of the one language by the word which you conceive to be its equivalent in the other. How few, even among us non-Babbitts, can keep themselves continually on the alert for thoughts and their corresponding national symbols in print or in speech! Yet eternal vigilance is the price of mastery. "Watch, remember, repeat!" is the only motto. To learn French means to be forever snatching at the Frenchman's phrases as they emerge, and forever imitating them.

Like the confusion of word and thought is the confusion of spelling and word. As the word is the clothing of the idea, so is orthography the clothing of the word. "Simplifiers hold meeting to reform English language," announces a newspaper heading. One might as well call a convention of hatters a campaign to alter heads. Spelling is of course only an accepted visual symbol of something that is really of the ear and the mind. There are good hats and bad hats; for convenience' sake we usually prefer the style which the fashion of the day happens to prescribe. But changing a man's hat does not change his head, although, I admit, it may make a considerable difference in his appearance. Even so, an unaccustomed way of writing may at first sight give a word a strange character. Really to know a word, however, you must learn to apprehend it as an entity distinct from its conventional garment. Supposing you saw a man always in the same hat: that headpiece might become in your mind an essential part of his personality; you could not think of him in different headgear — still less could you picture him as hatless; and if you met him in a new hat you might fail to recognize him. It is just as well to catch sight of an acquaintance from time to time in unhabitual head-covering, or even with none at all. Which means (coming down from metaphor to literalness) that it is illuminating for us learners to see vocables sometimes decked out, let us say, in phonetic spelling, and, if we can, to get the knack of apprehending them directly by ear, without association with letters. Only after we shall have become thus familiar with them, I believe, can we claim them as our intimates. The naked sound is, for eye-workers, hard to conceive, though not so hard as the naked idea. Both of them, no doubt, make their best appeal without our consciousness; yet the successful student must acquire the art of abstracting at will.

There are several reasons why we pronounce alien languages so badly. One, perhaps the principal one, is our dependence on letters. I need not tell you that letters — all of them merely temporal and local conventional signs — have different functions in different languages. The letter u means one thing in German, another in French; the letter z means one thing to a Spaniard, another thing to an Englishman. And we have all of us been bred in our own national and contemporary association of sounds and letters. Until one has actually taught German, one cannot believe how difficult it is to convince pupils that German *die* and English *die* are not identical in sound. You may repeat the statement hundreds of times, you may howl yourself hoarse in oral demonstration; you may savagely threaten that the next boy who says *dy* must suit the action to the word. At the very end of the year there will still be pupils who cannot refrain from mortuary interpretation of the definite article. If that is the teacher's experience in one of the simplest of things linguistic, how can we expect beginners to inhibit themselves from sounding an *n* with the French nasal vowels, how can we expect them to believe that even in so beautifully spelled a language as Italian an accent mark on a final vowel letter really means something, or that the doubling of a consonant letter has a literal significance? Red-hot irons would not induce a whole class of pupils to pronounce *cantò* differently from *canto* or to make any difference between *pena* and *penna*. A double *n* in English means only (if it means anything) that the vowel before it is short: witness *penny*. An accent mark on a vowel symbol in French does not indicate that the vowel in question is stressed. In one respect, the student of several languages is worse off than one who knows only his own, for he has, to confuse him, the multiple alphabetic eccentricities of various badly spelled tongues. Really there would seem to be no salvation, unless it lie in teaching pronunciation first, and the conventional orthography considerably later.

I am not now discussing niceties of foreign utterance. I have in mind only the roughest approximation, sufficiently proximate, however, to be understood and not to expose the speaker to derision. With good-will, with patience, with intelligent and unswerving instruction, and especially with faith, one can do a little better than that; but the hope of an impeccable foreign accent is an illusion. Not that one should ever cease striving for perfection; illusions are given us for our betterment. One's ideal is not realized; what ideal is? But what does it matter? A tinge of the exotic does no harm; it may even lend a bit of pleasing color to one's speech. I know many a foreigner whose English is all the more delightful for not exactly reproducing our homespun. It is often declared that no adult can attain real perfection in a foreign idiom. I have forgotten what clever Frenchman once said concerning generalities: "All general statements are false, including this one." With this qualification, one may accept the damnation of the adult; except that linguistically adult age begins at twelve or so. At 25 one has quite as good a chance as at 15.

I have said that the greatest obstacle to oral triumph is the association of sound with spelling.

If we had a phonetic orthography for all our languages, that obstacle would largely disappear; and, even though we have it not, the use of a phonetic notation signally mitigates the horrors of the novitiate in language study. The next drawback is the persistence of mental habits — grooves in the mind, or paths in the brain, as psychologists call them. We unwittingly connect certain sounds with certain muscular sensations. The sensation may suggest the sound, or the sound the sensation — oftener the latter. But the number of sounds within the province of the unilingual person is limited, and proportionately restricted is his stock of accustomed sensations. Each audible unit in his repertory has its own set of muscular associates, and does not willingly wander outside the home circle. Now let a new sound intrude: what happens? The brain, if it recognizes the sound as new, is at a loss how to place it. The familiar performances of the muscles are inadequate, and the poor brain knows no others. Perhaps it is not even aware that a stranger is in the pew; at any rate, it gives the outsider the place of one of its regular parishioners, and calls in the muscular services that belong of right to the old pew-holder. To put it concretely in the form of an example, if the German word *ach* is for the first time heard by an Englishman or an Italian, the listener may simply hear the *ch* as a *k* — rather an odd *k*, to be sure,

but one to be reproduced by the familiar *k* procedure; he says *ak*, and goes on his way rejoicing. Or,
if the stranger's grain-grooves are not so petrified,
he is conscious that *ach* is not *ak*, but, having had
no experience with *ch*, and having at his disposal
no means of producing it, he substitutes for it the
nearest sound in his stock, and pronounces *ak* as
the first man did, though not with the same satisfaction. Thus in either case the foreign sound is
replaced by a native one. Society is divided into
two groups: firstly, those who use, let us say, *k* for
ch and do not know the difference; secondly, those
who perceive a difference but use *k* just the same,
because they do not know what else to do.

One might point out here the utility of a course in
practical phonetics — that is, a full series of exercises in unfamiliar sounds, developing their sensational accompaniments. Such development can be
speeded by description of the vocal organs and how
they perform, but it can be achieved without this
rational background, provided pupils be very
young or have a "good ear." A "good ear": that
is the essential. It means retardation of the fossil-
izing of the brain into a small number of aural and
muscular associations. It means the habit of
quickly creating new paths of communication when
new sounds are heard or new sounds are to be produced. A "good ear" is a gift of God. But, like all
God's gifts, it needs cultivation, and it can be cul-

tivated. You are familiar with the power of the accustomed eye to see things which to the novice are invisible. I doubt whether the Indian or the backwoodsman has by nature a better eye than you; he sees better because he has formed the habit of doing so, the habit of drawing swift and sure inferences from minute data. The old salt feels more accurately than you the direction of the wind, not because his cheek is tenderer, but because he knows the exact value of a small stimulus. So you, as you progress in yachtsmanship, come to feel the relation between any grade of pressure on wheel or tiller and the direction of the boat.

The first requisite is an open mind. That is the secret of expertness in any line; it is the secret of the "good ear." The bad-eared people are those who, having their perception all divided up into compartments, close their minds to anything that does not fit into one of their pigeon-holes. When they encounter a novelty, they either ignore it, or, if they cannot, into a pigeon-hole it must go, willy-nilly. Here, doubtless, the superiority complex enters into the game. For Mr. Podsnap, the difference between the Frenchman's speech and his own is due to the French inability to speak as the English do. If we are to trust English novelists, the pigeon-holed type of mind is particularly common in England. That type, wherever it occur, will never learn anything new, unless it accomplish the hard task of breaking down its compartments. The "good ear" is constant openness, constant willingness to admit the unknown, constant alertness to recognize the value of small stimuli. With recognition of unfamiliar differences in acoustic effect comes quick groping for means to reproduce them. And the search, if confident, is almost sure to be rewarded. That is what we mean, in acoustic matters, by "imitation."

But here a new obstacle presents itself. Giant Despair rises up in our path. "By Despair," says St. Thomas (quoting from St. Isidore), "we go down into hell." Truly it is so in the conquest of language. I have already said that conviction of our impotence to do a thing makes us impotent. "To despair is to go down into hell." By Hope alone, verdant Hope, may we be saved. And Hope — remember this! — Hope, theologically speaking, does not mean "perhaps": it means assurance of success. To imitate, we must believe that we can imitate; and, if we believe, we can. Consider the case of a new sound, or a new combination, confronting a novice. He is already advanced enough on his way to the Celestial City to recognize it as new. "I cannot do it," he cries. Despair seizes him; and I need not tell you where he will go. "Anyhow," he puffs, in self-excuse, "it is not English, and consequently is beneath the notice of a true Englishman or a hundred-percent American." Thus the superiority complex and the inferiority complex combine for his damnation. Faith must come to the rescue of Hope. We must believe, not only that we can do it, but also that it is worth doing — that we *must* do it. And if, long before this, charity has whispered her sweet incentive, we are saved. With open mind, with power to register and control our sensations, with confidence that we possess the means of imitation, we have won the battle. We are captains of our souls.

Thus far, I have addressed myself to the pupil rather than to the teacher. Many of you are both. So am I; so I have been during most of my life. Long experience in both capacities impels me to emphasize a maxim which we all feel to be true, but which none of us admit. The maxim is this: never make a mistake — or, if you are a teacher, never allow your pupils to make a mistake. When I say "never," I of course mean what Captain Corcoran meant. But the principle is the same, and it is an important principle, in that it runs counter to all the Rousseauistic doctrine of education. According to Jean-Jacques, we learn by our mistakes. Emile's admirable tutor works overtime to dig a hole for his pupil to fall into, his principle being that we learn to avoid holes only by tumbling into them. And his doctrine has more or less permeated all nineteenth century pedagogy. Reluctant though I be to oppose such authority, I must confess that I do not believe a word of it. If Emile had once fallen into that hole, he would always have fallen into it; for whomever else we imitate or fail to imitate, we eternally imitate ourselves. Half a century ago, when I first came to Cambridge, Massachusetts, I mixed up Concord Avenue and Garden Street; and although I have lived in the immediate neighborhood of Garden Street (or is it Concord Avenue?) ever since, I always have to stop to think which is which. Have you ever looked up a word in the dictionary? And, if so, have you ever used that word again without looking it up afresh? This very day I opened my Webster for the word *dullness*. I cannot say what process of introspection suggested that word to me; but I wanted to know whether to spell it with one *l* or two. Of course I discovered it may be written either way; it always turns out like that. Yet of one thing I am sure: if I ever have occasion to use the word *dullness* (or *dulness*) again, I shall again open my Webster; and so on until the crack of doom. My only safety lies in avoiding the word forevermore. So many words, however, have been thus eliminated from my vocabulary that my resources are becoming perceptibly inadequate.

I have heard that a woman's first love is never forgotten, but always lurks in her thoughts, however numerous and potent may have been its successors. There is, I fancy, a dominance in anything which in our experience is first. The first mountain you ever saw, your first sea voyage, your first trip by rail or by air: these are the things that remain in your memory, when all else is blank or blur. Read a book three times, four times, at intervals of ten years. At the end of it all, what do you retain of that book? Just what you got out of it at the first reading. Your subsequent repetitions may reinforce that primal impression, but they add to it nothing permanent. I have a friend who once lived at No. 15 on a certain street; he now lives at No. 8, and has lived there for twenty years, whereas he lived only one year at No. 15. Yet every time I write to him — two or three times a week — I check my hand just in the act of writing "15." Which shoe do you put on first, the right or the left? Presumably the one which you selected the first time you ever wore shoes. If Emile's tutor, on the day of the momentous experiment, had, by suggestion, argument, or even by a brutal shove, prevented his ingenuous pupil from precipitating himself into that cavity, the disciple never would have developed the hole-seeking proclivity, the entire course of his life would have been different, and man, taking thought of his peril (rather than *at* his peril), would never have become a depraved animal.

The epithet "depraved animal" is one which you would dearly love to hurl at the members of an elementary class when, after studying under your ex-

pert guidance for a year, they have just offered
you, in loving testimony of their profit, their final
examination in the subject. Somewhere the sun is
shining; but in you there is no joy, and Mudville is
your home town. For that examination paper will
prove to be an aggregation of all the first mistakes
of the year. The first time your disciple met such
and such a word, he mistranslated it; the first time
he formed a plural, he made it wrong; the first time
he used a certain tense, he muffed it. And in spite
of all correction, in spite of reformation, in spite of
apparent emancipation from all sinful practices,
when it comes to the final reckoning, that pupil's
sins will find him out. At that awful moment they
all rise up before him; they fill his whole field of
vision; his entire paper is a confession of original
sin — original, that is to say, not in the historical
but in the personal sense. Theoretically, at least,
all this wickedness (or a good part of it) might have
been avoided, and the class saved. If, at the crucial
instant, some one had appeared on the scene and
shot Emile's tutor, what a different contribution
to human felicity the arts and sciences might have
made!

All this you know from experience, whether in
the active or the passive voice. But even if you
did not, the abstract idea would be found self-
evident, were you not afraid of Emile's tutor. If
that sapient gentleman's views were correct, what

would be his use in the world? What would be the use of parents or masters or guardians? If everybody is to learn everything by himself, the elder's occupation would seem to be gone. Or shall the only mature survivors be gravediggers, whose one business shall be to provide receptacles for the indiscretions of youth? Could one carry to completion that principle of unassisted self-teaching, humanity would obviously never advance, because one generation could not be allowed to impart to another the fruit of its experience. And since inheritance of acquired characters is forbidden also, progress would be successfully excluded: either we must forever trudge in the same treadmill, or, as is likelier, we must revert to the noble savage—which, no doubt, is the most beautiful thing that could happen to us.

At that prospect, however, be not unduly elated nor unduly alarmed. No human power is ever going to prevent the old from telling the young all they know, and considerably more. Only let the ancient strive so to live and so to think and speak and write as to suggest to their juniors the most efficacious of all modes of learning: imitation.

DIFFICILIOR LECTIO

The boast of heraldry, the pomp of pow'r
And all that beauty, all that wealth e'er gave
Awaits alike the inevitable hour:
The paths of glory lead but to the grave.

GENERALLY printed and always recited with "await" instead of "awaits," although "awaits," I am sure, has the better authority. But supposing it had not; supposing the rival turns were equally supported: how should one decide? That is the occasion on which an expert invokes the principle of the *difficilior lectio,* or harder reading. For the presumption is that a change from hard to easy is more in accordance with human habits than a change from easy to hard. Assuming that Gray, classical scholar that he was, wrote "awaits," with "hour" as the subject, the deformation into a more commonplace arrangement, with the subject in the lead, is almost as "inevitable" as death's "hour"; and "await" ensues. If, on the other hand, he had put "awaits," the spouter and the printer, too literary to write a plural subject with a verb in the singular, but not literary enough to recognize in the "boast" and the "pomp," and all the rest, an object and not a subject, would have been sure to substitute "await." And so, no doubt, it happened.

It is evident that the determining principle has twice come into play. Starting with "awaits," the semi-competent repeater takes the verb to be an "easy" form, because "all" (the portion of the apparent subject immediately preceding it) is singular; therefore he corrects to "await," which from his point of view is the "harder" and therefore the likelier version. Then, after a sufficient predominance of "await," appears the trained critic, who, recognizing "awaits" as really the harder, because it transposes the usual order of words, restores it to its primacy.

My point is that the notion of the *difficilior lectio* is not confined to philologists. It is inborn. With them, to be sure, it is formally recognized and consciously applied, while the layman applies it unknowingly. In making this statement I am not harboring the Platonic heresy of "innate ideas": even St. Thomas admits that certain *principia* are born with us, and this, I take it, is one of them. Why else should boys say "sweet firm" for "sweet fern"? Nearly all did, when I was one of them. We knew that shrub, we loved its fragrance; we dried its foliage and smoked it, and "fern" was our middle name. Why "firm" then, except that "fern" seemed too obvious? No doubt a similar obviousness is responsible for the transformation of "poison ivy" into "poison ivory."

By the way, did you ever, in middle life, try to resuscitate boyhood's ecstasies by indulging in the perfumed vice of fern-smoking? I did. After dallying with the thought a long time, I decided the hour had come. Having collected and carefully dried the odorant leaves, eagerly and with exquisite care I fashioned the dainty cigarettes — fabricated, not with newspaper as of old, but with elegant note-paper. Then, luxuriously couched on the verandah, dreaming of "les roses d'Ispahan," I struck fire and inhaled the first whiffs. . . . No; I do not want to be a boy again. One moment of juvenile entrancement was enough; ah! how shall I tell how much more than enough! How can such abundance of nausea dwell in so small and so sweet a plant? My Eden vanished with the first taste of the wood. Adam-like, I resignedly took my solitary way down the path of life.

Yet this experience brings us no closer to the usurpation of "firm." There is no escaping the conclusion that it is purely and simply a case of the *difficilior lectio*: "sweet firm" must be right because it means nothing. *Credo quia absurdum.*

A half century and more ago, the most prevalent types of dog were the Newfoundland and the black-and-tan; for dogs, like everything else, are subject to the whim of fashion. We children used to call the smaller variety "black'n'tan," as everybody else did. But there was one particularly knowing small boy who said "black battan," riming with "rattan." Where he got this monstrous vocable, I cannot imagine; but little by little it became mysteriously impressive. All of us treated it with respect, and the most daring among us adopted it. Harder; therefore presumably revealed.

> Old man driving cattle;
> Don't you hear his money rattle?
> One, two, three,
> Out goes he!

That is a perfectly good formula, efficacious and sanctioned by tradition. Why, then, should some children alter "cattle" into "castle," spoiling both rime and sense? When certain rime-greedy innovators sang

> I'm Captain Jinks of the Horse Marinks
> I feed my horse on corn and beans,

one could understand (without approving) the impatience which led to the creation of "Marinks," unwilling to await the lawful union of "marines" and "beans." But "Old man driving castle" is not only meaningless but rimeless. Its sole recommendation is its total lack of motive. Yet the users of that version were in my day regarded with peculiar tolerance — nay, with a sort of veneration, as probable initiates in a mystic cult. Such is the

esoteric implication of a phrase devoid of significance. What is more potent or more persistent
than a slogan which means nothing at all, in games,
in politics, in society, in philosophy, in religious
dogma? In addition to the suggestion of an inner
shrine, there is in meaninglessness the advantage of
impregnability. Who shall impugn the inerrancy
of a formula which nobody understands because
there is nothing in it?

I think I have already discussed somewhere the
strange fate that has overtaken the protective
charm,

> Sticks and stones
> May break my bones,
> But names will never hurt me.

This spell is used, of course, as an antidote to vitu-
peration. But what becomes of its efficacy when
"names" is altered to "nails," as occasionally
happens? Can anyone tell me how nails ever were
pounded into it? Once inserted, they were bound
to cling, for they had the requisite irrelevancy.

After all, though, names are pretty adhesive.
We all of us declare, with bromidical reminiscence,
that a rose by any other name would smell as
sweet; but would it? I have my doubts, especially
when I remember how the word for "rose," in
French and Italian, has been miraculously preserved from the ordinary phonetic alterations;
for the flower, in French, would normally be called

"reuse." Again, that "salt sea smell" owes its bracing effect to its sturdily alliterative appellation. It would be far less health-giving if we knew that its peculiar quality comes from rotten seaweed. Twenty-five years ago, when automobiles were just beginning to be omnipresent and the pervasive stench of gasoline was a new and intolerable plague, I sought refuge in a suburban meadow. There, drawing in long breaths of pure country air, I became conscious of a particularly rural fragrance, aromatic, intoxicating, irresistible in its suggestion of waste and wild. "What can it be," I cried, "this emanation of the fields that fills the air with its perfume?" Not until I had said all that, and more too, did I recognize the trail of the skunk.

Skunks are pretty little beasts, gentle and considerate. They are said to make ideal pets, but I have never tested their qualifications in that capacity. I do feel an attachment, however, for one of the family. Here is how it happened. Three of us chaps were out exploring, along the banks of Little River. Cautiously we proceeded, in single file, close together. I was in the lead; next came a large man, "deep-bosomed," like Homer's ladies; the third was long and lean. I had just lifted my foot for another step, when immediately under it I espied a bright-eyed bunch of black and white. With automatic recoil I instantly plunged deep into the deep bosom of number two; and he, thus taken unawares, toppled crushingly back on number three. While we lay in a helpless heap, the skunk, with a smile in which friendliness mingled with amusement, softly slipped away; but, like the Bald'insville Fire Brigade in Artemus Ward's story, he "kindly refrained from squirtin'."

In legend and in looks, skunks are eternally related to kittens. This relationship may excuse the introduction of a kitten at this point. A pure white kitten, slender, big-eared, one eye blue and the other yellow, graceful, affectionate, sportive and dangerously innocent. So innocent was she, in fact, that she had never even heard of dogs. Well, one evening some friends called, with a yellow setter — an example to all setters, gentle, domestic and accustomed to cats as household companions. We were all curious to see what would happen when the two animals met. Presently the fluffy little creature entered the room. On beholding the setter, she registered first amazement, then curiosity in conflict with apprehension. In a moment, however, curiosity won the day. Slowly approaching, she seated herself in front of the sitting stranger; then, standing on her hind legs, she softly took his muzzle between her front paws, and touched noses. A brief revulsion followed — a withdrawal under a chair; an arched, bristling back, even a faint hissing sound. Soon, however, she was back again, playing with the tip of the dog's tail. This affront to his dignity was borne patiently for a while; but at last the owner of the tail arose, tucked that article tightly between his hind legs, and, with a deprecating glance at the company, sat down again.

Whence comes the conventional hostility between dogs and cats? Is it innate, like the principle of the *difficilior lectio*, or is it acquired, like a taste for cinnamon toast or an admiration for Modigliani? Of course the same question arises with regard to our horror of snakes. Speaking of snakes and cats, why does a cat, when she catches a snake, carry it up on your piazza and eat its head off, leaving the decapitated body on the floor, as Judith left Holofernes? She (the cat, I mean) does the same with a rat, or a mouse. One summer we took our cat — a citified middle-aged one — to the seashore, where she developed into an expert huntress, strewing our verandah with her acephalous trophies. With crabs, however, she had no success, although she made many a persistent attempt; on the other hand, she met with no nipping defeat. Crabs intrigued her — as she would have said, had she lived today. But my problem is this: do cats prefer the head of their prey for the pleasure of the palate or because its consumption gives them a supreme sense of triumph? I can hardly think of a rat's head as a delicacy; but, then, I am not a cat. Presumably we all take a certain satisfaction in eating what we kill. Once, as a small boy, I caught an eel; and, repulsive though it looked, I insisted on devouring it (cooked, of course). I have never eaten one since; and, even that time, I did not eat the head. Some savages, I am told, make a practice of devouring divers parts of a slain enemy, expecting thereby to acquire a portion of the foeman's fighting capacity. I wonder whether my cat, when she crunched the snake's head, was hoping to absorb the cunning of the subtil beast. Rats, too, are conspicuously intelligent, as well as brave; and for that reason their brains may be worth assimilating. In favor of the other explanation may be cited the look of perfect self-approval which lights the countenance of a cat when she has performed her head-eating rite. Often she will bring you the remainder of her victim for your admiring inspection. As far as I can remember, my own emotion in consuming the eel was a sense of victory achieved beyond recall. I surely had no thought of winning an increase of slipperyness. But what is the use of speculating? These questions of motive are insoluble. The likelihood is that the less likely answer is the likelier one.

Questions of ethics are just as baffling. For instance, which is the more immoral creature, the brute who in a crowd treads on your heel, or the moron in front on whose heel you step? Here I can

see no solution; between two superlatives there is
no choice. Both are equally hard and equally easy,
according to your point of view.

"Willy," said the Sunday School teacher, "if
you picked up on the street a nickel that was not
yours, would you keep it?" "Gosh, no!" answered
Willy, "I'd buy an ice cream cone." Was he right
or wrong? "Wrong," of course, is the obvious
reply. But is it not too obvious? Can "wrong" be
right? Supposing Willy, unable to find the owner,
after notice to the police and due advertising in the
newspapers, had put the nickel into the missionary
box, it would probably have gone to some heathen
country where ice cream cones are unknown, and
would thus have been wasted. And what is wick-
eder than economic waste?

That is an inquiry that comes home to roost.
"It's a dam poor sermon that don't hit me somewhere," as the feller said. By the way, I once wrote
an essay on that subject — not the "dam poor
sermon," but the phrase "as the feller said,"
which some folks about here attach as a *clausula*
to every statement they make. "The summer
people blame me for cuttin' down them spruce
trees. But what can I do about it? My money's in
it, as the feller said." This I heard only a few days
ago. But a great many days and a great many
years ago the habit was already rife. Do you remember Farquhar's play, *The Beaux' Stratagem*? I

didn't remember it until I saw it in revival last autumn; and then I noticed that Boniface, the landlord, ends every one of his utterances with the tag, "as the saying is." Now, did my spruce-cutters and fish-catchers get the trick from Farquhar? Not being a specialist in tracing literary derivations, I choose the easier way, and declare that they did not. But presumably I am wrong.

Returning to the sinfulness of economic waste, as the saying is, I must explain my implication that my own conscience is scarred with that sin. I was young, to be sure, but not young enough to excuse my iniquity, somewhere in the early thirties, I think. And I was indulging in my favorite pastime of rowing a dory, off Duxbury beach. On the one side, the endless stretch of sandy shore; on the other, the broad Atlantic. For years, I made it a practice thus to plough the ocean for two hours every day, no matter what the weather might be. Were it not for fear of swerving from my subject, I could tell tales of crashing storms, of foamy surf-riding, of occasional disturbance of the normal respective positions of boat and boatman; but I must hurry on. That particular day was calm and bright. So still, indeed, was the sea that I was half dozing, when all at once I noticed on the beach, not a quarter of a mile away, an elderly gentleman dancing violently, in absolute solitude. Had he been a bather, I might have imagined that a crab had attached itself to his toe. But, no: he was fully dressed, and elegantly. His angular movements, quite out of accord with the rotundity of his figure, did not suggest a "daily dozen." Temperament, rather than Hygiene, seemed to lurk behind them. As I slowly approached, it appeared to me that he was vigorously shouting, and I half suspected that he was trying to attract my attention; but I could hear nothing. Little by little, I got the idea that his gestures had as their focus a certain spot in the Atlantic. I, too, then concentrating my scrutiny in that direction, discerned a minute white speck afar out on the gently swaying blue. To my quick intelligence it occurred that perhaps the lonely gentleman's saltations had some mysterious connection with the white dot. Cautiously I approached it. With a quick, daring thrust I effected a capture, and discovered that my prey was a new Panama hat, which, after a considerable shoreward pull, I restored to the owner on the end of an oar. What a beautiful thing is gratitude! With an impulse which he might later have regretted, the erstwhile hatless but now happily hatted disciple of Terpsichore extracted from his trousers pocket a dime and a nickel, which, smilingly, he held out to me. Here comes the tragedy. An insane pride — "by that sin fell the angels" — a mad pride moved me to refuse the gift. Courteously, I hope, but decisively, I know, the offering was gestured away; and, turning my back on the reunited couple, I once more set my face to the rising sun.

This is rather a long story, but it is true; and its theme is economic waste, the folly and the sinfulness of it. When you think of what fifteen cents, in those days, could buy! Often, often, in the arid stretches of after-life, I have dreamt of those fifteen cents, as the fevered patient dreams of cool springs. No "harder lesson" have I learned.

But a truce to moralizing, and especially to self-pity! My friend, Irving Babbit, would have told me I was becoming a humanitarian; and nothing can be worse than that. "Harder lessons" still may await me. Call no man happy until he is dead. "Have you lived all your life here?" said a humanitarian tourist to the oldest inhabitant of a poverty-stricken village. "Not yit," was the answer. Still, I cannot help wondering, sometimes, what my life would have been if my mother's wish had been fulfilled and I had become a clergyman. One must not draw too conclusive deductions from a tendency to moralize. Remember the Emperor Galba, who, according to Tacitus, would have seemed to possess all the requisites for an Emperor — if he had never been one.

Self-pity: worse than useless, but so easy! When George Sandford had a hard task to perform, I am sure that, instead of considering how miserable he was, he forthwith set himself to discover some as-

pects of his business that might be interesting.
And I dare say there are in every job some features
that are interesting, at any rate to a fertile mind.
A tiny negro boy I once saw was engaged in loading
a little cart with a lot of wood that was too big for
it. Piled over high, the pieces tumbled out as soon
as the vehicle started. Again and again he tried,
sadness on his brow. Always the same result, and
always the same despondency. Finally his eye
brightened; he had an idea. Taking all the wood
out, he ingeniously packed it, stick by stick, until
the load fitted exactly and securely. Then he
looked up, and I greeted him with a word of admiration. Have you ever, on a dark night, seen the
full moon suddenly break through the clouds? If
so, you can imagine the dazzling flash of white
teeth in a black face.

That transformation was a symbol of the changes
in human moods. It reminded me of one summer's
day in my childhood when, introverting, I first
began to divine the flux of my own states of mind.
Puzzling, disconcerting, more and more alarming
the longer I studied, were the quick alternations of
gladness and gloom. One moment, all cheerful-
ness; the next, without apparent reason, a sudden
melancholy. An obvious though rather terrifying
explanation presented itself in the form of a theory
of mysterious vapors in my brain. Then something
moved me to look outward, and I presently dis-

covered that my periods of depression coincided with the passages of clouds between the sun and myself. By nature we are all sun-worshipers, I suppose; at any rate, I was one. And every time the luminary was veiled, my moral mercury went down. Repeated experience convinced me of the truth of this remoter solution of the problem, and after that the variations of my inner thermometer caused me no serious alarm. Yet even now I have my bed so placed, summer and winter, that the sun shall shine on my face as soon as it rises.

Is it the Puritan blood in us that inclines to introspection? Anyhow, it often happens that phenomena which we attribute to some hidden internal deterioration, physical or moral, may be traced to a prosaic concrete cause without. For a long period I suffered from a prickling in my left elbow and a numbness of the whole forearm. Though not constant, it was with me most of the time, except during vacations. As years went on, it worried me more and more and my thoughts turned to creeping paralysis. Anxiety might, indeed, have driven me into hypochondria, had I not fortunately made the observation that I had acquired, in the intensity of talking, reading, and writing, the habit of digging my left elbow into the arm of my chair or the edge of my table. The discovery relieved my mind, but the cure involved resort to armless chairs, which I still have reason to prefer. Again, in my late forties, I began to be troubled by sharp headaches, which would come on after bicycling and on awakening in the morning. Never having been subject to such annoyances before, I came to regard it as one of the necessary ills of advancing age, and prepared myself to accept it with resignation. Not until I had observed in my glass, with some surprise, the rapid denudation of the once thickly forested area on my cranium did it occur to me that the ache might be connected with the use of a transparently thin riding-cap and the nightly proximity of my bare head to a wide-open window. Since then, the megrim has not returned. For the Puritan, or near-Puritan, the easier — that is, the more instinctive — reading is to be found in the book of subjectivity. That sounds rather pedantic, but I fancy there is some truth in it; its very difficulty creates a presumption in its favor.

Here is a problem that recently confronted me in semi-Puritan territory. Paddling about the bay, I came upon a fishing-boat, white with a recent coat of paint. It had no name, only a number. But, as I looked closely, I could easily discern under the fresh pigment the name "Pauline." Mystery! Why had the owner painted out Pauline? Here is food for a dozen conjectures, of various degrees of unlikelihood. Perhaps the simple fisherman's beloved, on whom he had built all his hopes, even to the extent of naming his boat for her, had changed her mind and refused to marry him; and he, in bitterness, by expunging her from his craft had vainly attempted to expunge her from his memory. Or, possibly, Pauline had become his wife and — worse tragedy still — had failed to meet his expectation. Think what a constant and galling mockery that name on the stern must have been! In his daily thought and his daily conversation the hated word must automatically recur. Never could he refer to his occupation without mention of his undutiful spouse. At last, in desperation, with one agonized sweep of the brush, the unendurable reminder disappeared — or nearly disappeared; for, as I said, I could plainly read it through the paint. Thus, no doubt, despite all effort to remove it her image was still graven on his heart. Another guess: let us assume that the boatman had a literary bent and had attempted to read Robert Browning's earliest masterpiece. With the hopeful enthusiasm of youth, he had inscribed on his vessel the title of that poem before he had actually begun its perusal; and in aged disillusion had effaced the name when he finally gave up the job. This theory, I submit, is improbable enough to merit serious consideration. Still one more: there is a law compelling boats to bear an official letter and number, and inasmuch as the owner, when he repainted his craft, was obliged to denominate it B-41144, he may have thought that another name would be an extravagance and so have suppressed Pauline merely for economy. For my romantic temperament, this is the hardest explanation of all; and therefore, I reluctantly admit, the most probable.

I have already shown that the most difficult problems have to do with motives, with the secret wherefore. Let me, in conclusion, repeat an illustrative tale told recently by a college president at the Commencement afternoon alumni exercises of another college. But first I must tell another anecdote reported by the same narrator on the same occasion. "Are ye sufferin' much with your rheumatism, Si?" asked a kindly neighbor. "What the hell else can a man do with it?" replied Silas. This is scarcely a problem story, because the question involved admits of but one answer. It may, then, serve as a foil to the first mentioned incident, which is all one great interrogation point. Here is the scene. A sight-seeing lorry, in the north of England, is just drawing near an ancient building with an ancient sign-board, surrounded by ancient trees. "We are now," shouts the megaphone man, "passing by the oldest tavern in England." At that a drowsy American on the back seat starts up and plaintively demands: "Why?"

There it is! That eternally tempting and eternally baffling Why.

TEE UM LIE

"Excuse me, sir," said the polite little girl; "would you please tell me what time it was." The "was," of course, sounds funny; but why should it? We have in "was" merely an exemplification of the old rule of the sequence of tenses, which was so rubbed into us when we studied Latin and Greek and the modern tongues, even our native English. There may have been an exception, in fine print, that could be stretched to cover this case. But according to the long primer rule, "would," being a past tense, calls its dependent verb into the past. E.g., "he says you are an ass"; but "he said you were an ass." You may still be one, you know, but the narrator of the second story is referring only to the state of things at a bygone time, when some friend was making the friendly remark. I suppose you might, if you chose, invoke the authority of a footnote to the effect that statements eternally and universally true may be expressed in the present, even though the main verb be in the past. "He proved that the earth was round," or "is round" if you are perfectly sure of its rotundity. Thus a sufficiently well-informed person might say either: "he declared that you were an ass" or "he declared that you are an ass."

The "were" and the "was," and the whole principle of sequence of tenses, are manifestations of the deep-lying principle of "like likes like." We phrase it in sundry proverbs: "birds of a feather flock together," "a man is known by the company he keeps," "like master, like man." In the grammarians' elucidation of syntactical niceties much subtle logic is expended, and much psychological ingenuity, whereas I fancy many of them, far from being the result of logical excogitation, come from sheer blind imitativeness, a consequence of association. To follow well-worn paths through the brain is easier than to strike out in new ones.

The tendency to association and the resultant habit of assimilation make for harmony, and, if carried further on, for monotony. Revolt against their domination when tyranny becomes too oppressive may, if led by a great pioneer, start new currents in language, art, industry, or thought. If, on the other hand, the revolters be themselves infertile, as is generally the case, the outcome is petulant and puerile cacophony. Ripples which to the floating gnat look mountain-high disappear in the broad expanse of the stream. "When will the public realize," shrieked an hysterical reviewer a couple of years ago, "that the publication of

Joyce's *Ulysses* is a far more important event than the World War?" And already the reader scratches his head and asks himself: "Let me see! What was Joyce's *Ulysses*?"

That past tense brings me back to my linguistic theme, from which I was in danger of straying. The things which we call "assimilation," "analogy," "euphony" are all products of the grouping tendency that is a part of our nature. Why do so many of our countrymen (of course not you and I) pronounce "gooseberry" with a z and "newspaper with an s? With most of our neighbors, if the truth be told, the first syllable of the latter word becomes simply "noose." Even the unphilological scarcely need to be told that the b of "gooseberry," being a sonant, turns the s of "goose" into its sonant mate z; whereas the surd p of "newspaper" reduces the sonant final of "news" to its surd partner. Such changes, representing a resort to familiar brain-paths and economy of muscle-moving, are going on about us, and in us, all the time. There is one effective check on them: the desire to be understood; for that, in general, is the purpose of speech.

Unless the thing said is unexpected (which rarely happens in ordinary converse), a bare suggestion suffices to convey the meaning. "Maw" signifies "good morning," and "nigh" does for "good night." Does "tee um lie" mean anything to you?

That was the most satisfactory item in my inter-course with little Eddie, my only human playmate for many a week. I suppose he was three and I was six. At any rate, he seemed to me distressingly immature. He was, I think, a good little boy, but his intelligible discourse was limited to "tee um lie." Really I much preferred the company of his dog, a Newfoundland named Ben, who, although he could not talk at all, could put across things of much greater variety and importance than "tee um lie." How Ben and I did cling to each other! What wrestling matches we had, and what chases across the field! Little Eddie could do none of these things. All he could do was to make fantastic and futile attempts at self-expression, culminating in "tee um lie." Still, he was better, perhaps, than nobody. In my affection, I think he stood midway between Ben and my mud-turtle. This latter companion would have gained a stronger hold on my heart if he had not so promptly and so un-gratefully run away, just after I had made him the beautifullest little pen, with a little pool, a few ferns, and some tufts of moss. Perhaps there was not mud enough.

All this happened in Worcester, where I was visiting an aunt. It was so long ago that the Boston and Albany tracks ran across the Common, and the Station, black and grimy, was on Front Street. Of course there was no Union Station;

people changed at Worcester Junction, some distance out of town. An old country tavern stood on the site of the first "Union Depot" that Worcester knew, and across the way was a saloon kept by a man (a clear case of predestination) with the strangely prophetic name of Rumhole. In one corner of the Common was a colony of guinea pigs — or were they prairie dogs? Absorbingly interesting creatures, anyhow.

Later, my aunt lived on the top of the hill. Then it was wintertime, and on that summit I had no companion except a dead squirrel which a neighbor shot and brought home. Even in death its eyes were bright; and how soft its fur was against one's face! I played with it until the family declared that the smell (purely imaginary, I thought) was unendurable. Then I had to bury my pet — no easy task, for the ground was frozen. Subsequently I discovered a couple of boys, inferior to my squirrel-friend at every point, except perhaps in odoriferousness.

I went to school, too; but I cannot tell whether it was for a week, a month, or a season. It is just a shapeless shudder. I remember the building, which is still there; of teachers and pupils, nothing whatever. I wonder whether other people have such blank spots in their memories, similar to the black holes in the sky, which, astronomers now believe, are not emptiness but intervening opaque matter.

In my case, the dark screen would seem to be a merciful veil of horror. Just one little scene comes back to me. In the School yard. Having got a particle of coal into my eye, I am roaming about distressfully seeking solitude. All around me crowd goblin-like boys with vacant faces and great goggle-eyes, who point me out to one another, chanting monotonously: "There's a feller's got a lickin'." Vehemently I protest, explaining the real cause of my tearfulness. After a while the idea penetrates. The crowding and pointing continue, to be sure, but the formula, though always in the same color-less tone, has its text altered: "There's a feller's got som'p'm' in his eye."

But I must return to my aunt's earlier habitat, the abode of Eddie and Ben. It is on a hillside and has an atmosphere of spring and youthful summer. Toward the close of a long day, leaning against a fence, I overhear, in an adjacent field, a little girl singing to her still smaller companions a long bal-lad about a fire. It was my first taste of balladry. Vaguely I remember how the conflagration raged from strophe to strophe. The last stanza, as nearly as I can recall it after sixty years, ran something like this:

> But it was my opinion,
>   And I'm of the opinion still,
> That the fire broke out on the other side,
>   On the further side of the hill.

The only part of which I am absolutely sure is the phrase "I'm of the opinion still," whose judicial tone deeply impressed me, in the childish voice of the singer. I can even now hear snatches of the melody.

Other fresh experiences are connected with that spot. My aunt, a chirographic expert, initiates me into the mysteries of beautiful penmanship. She teaches me, also, how to make paper stars — not flat ones, but three-dimensional, outstanding and resplendent, if neatly constructed of stiff white paper after the correct rule. They can be fastened together to form various decorations. To save my neck, I cannot recover that formula now; and so, according to the utilitarian view of pedagogy, that part of my education was wasted. So, I fear, was my acquisition of the knack of making picture-frames out of varnished pine cones. On the other hand, I fancy I could still practice the craft of stuffing bed-ticks with hay, which was imparted by my uncle. In exchange therefor I was able to put my inborn taste for printing to a practical use by composing for him a sign informing the public of his willingness to render such service. As to the technique of harnessing a horse, which art I added to my possessions, that is now a remnant of a forgotten culture.

But I have not yet revealed — for the benefit of those who need it — the significance of "tee um lie."

At the bottom of that grassy hillside, far away, was an iron foundry; for Worcester, once a rural cattle-market, was developing into an industrial city. By day, there would arise from the foundry a strange noise, muffled at that distance, and a cloud of smoke. And by night, not exactly a pillar of fire, but a bright glow, such as the Neapolitan sees over Vesuvius; rhythmical, too, with intermittent bursts of flame. In the dusk of early spring, the mystery of the twilight hour was heightened by weird evidence of the great fire-breathing monster, always lurking below. So fascinating it was — so beautiful and at once so terrifying — that we children never tired of watching, and had to be dragged to bed. It was at such moments that Eddie and I really entered into spiritual communion. And then I could actually understand his language, when with a pale smile and an unwonted gleam in his eyes he would point downward and exclaim: "Tee um lie!"

For "tee um lie" means "see the light."

Eddie in his linguistic efforts carried simplification too far. So did James, who used "boh" for "railway train." On the other hand, Philip, who pronounced "Indian" for "engine," was a victim of laudable but excessive and mistaken striving for correctness. A similar desire, no doubt, impelled two little brothers, just embarking on the difficult business of speech, who for a while always said "goning" for "going," "comning" for "coming," "talkning" for "talking," and so on. Whence arose that *n* in all the present participles? It made one think of the attempt to introduce into our vocabulary a word "motorneer," to designate the motor-man, or driver, when electric trams first came into use. "Motorneer" is of course built on the model of "engineer" and perhaps "mountain-eer"; it was evidently invented by some amateur philologist who had failed to observe that in these latter words the *n* is a part of the basis, "engine" or "mountain," and not of the ending, which is -*eer*. Our "goning" and "comning" must have had their analogical starting-point too; but what on earth can it have been? If we cannot discover it, we shall have to call the *n* of "goning," like the *n* of *stand*, an "infix" — a none too satisfactory device for covering up our ignorance. The solution calls for a very close familiarity with the habits of our two young self-expressionists. As is the case with so many expressionists of their age, their self, if unrestricted, was frequently lacrimose; and for that reason they early became familiar with the repressive exclamations, "don't cry," and "stop whining." Now, in their dialect, "cry" became "fwy" and "whine" became "fwine"; and inas-much as "don't cry" and "stop whining" were regarded as equivalent commands, "fwining" came to be considered as the present participle of "fwy."

From this verb the mode of formation was extended to all others. Hence sprang the participial *n*-stem in a language unfortunately doomed to early disappearance. But similar analogies have left their mark on languages that have held their own. Children's speech will often show us in a few months the course of phenomena that have taken centuries to develop in the language of adults.

When I was editor of a learned quarterly, a professor of German sent me a long article — really big enough for a book — intended to prove that the consonant-shifts in the Germanic languages are due to the bibulous habits of the Teutons. This was long, long before the War. The author's idea was suggested by listening to a victim of delirium tremens, who, in the space of fifteen minutes, went through the complete series of the first and second sound-shifts. Now, for a convincing demonstration, the author would have had to make it clear: (*a*) that drinking was a more important element in Teutonic Ur-Kultur than in the civilization of shiftless races; and (*b*) that the Teutons, steadfast though they might be in potation, were shiftier than their neighbors in the treatment of consonants. Evidence on both these points being scanty, I was compelled to decline the interesting article.

A delirium tremens addict has, I suppose (I wish it understood that I am speaking purely from conjecture), no stimulus to conformity, since he is talking only for his own delectation. He may go as far as he pleases. The child, on the other hand, usually wishes to be understood, and comprehension becomes impossible if he deviates beyond a certain point. His spirit of innovation is checked, therefore, not only by natural imitativeness, but also by the law of diminishing returns. The same thing, in a slower way, is true of grown people, and of communities. The history of a language represents a compromise between human instability and the dread of isolation.

It is surprising, though, how far language can depart from standards of clearness, and from logical consecutiveness, without sacrificing intelligibility. Our literary idiom certainly requires a very generous margin of distinctness. When a schoolboy wrote in an essay, "The Indians pursue their warfare by hiding behind trees and then scalping them," his meaning is luminous, although his words do not seriously lend themselves to a literal interpretation. Here is a bunch of "howlers" recently reported by the London *Spectator*. "The Irish cut out lawyers of bog and make them into peat" suggests a sly dig by a critic of legal obscurantism; but the statement is perfectly clear without the help of satire. So "A volcano is a mountain with a creator at the top pouring out hot lava," carries well enough its surface message, admirable though it be as a subtle picture of the Fundamentalist conception of the Deity. When asked "Under what conditions does the fourth act of *Hamlet* open?" a pupil replied: "The fourth act of Hamlet opens immediately after the close of the third." Literalism can go no further.

But far better than any of these schoolboy performances are some of the concise rules for French grammar concocted by an American teacher of that language. These formulas had to be short enough to be snapped off in the classroom whenever demanded. "What's the rule for nasal *n*?" "When *n* is nasal it isn't pronounced" was the correct and only answer. Do not stop to ask yourself whether *n* is ever anything but nasal, or how any sound can be nasal if it isn't pronounced; just wonder at the brute force of this phrase, which, without saying anything at all, drives home its lesson. Here the transcendental so far transcends the literal as to make it needless.

Generally speaking, children are literalists, and so, to be sure, are most adults. My aunt, who in middle life was subject to severe headaches, used to keep as a remedy a small bottle of ammonia which she would hold gingerly to either nostril. This bottle I was warned never to open; one whiff of it would knock a man down. I did long to see the experiment tried; I longed to see a tall man unsuspectingly uncork the phial and all at once keel stiffly over, like a figure out of Noah's Ark. But I never, though of an inquiring mind, quite dared to be the guinea pig myself. Never yet have I opened a bottle of ammonia. I did, however, test at my own peril the reliability of various other warning statements. "Raisins will give you fits," said my aunt. "A little girl who had been told not to touch them climbed up to the top shelf and ate nearly half a pound of them. She died in frightful convulsions." The immediate result of this moral tale was the consumption of half a pound of raisins, which, unfortunately for my soul, did not disturb my bodily comfort. "Cherries and milk will kill you"; everybody told me that, my aunt among the rest. This experiment required some bracing, but I put it through. Furthermore, on obtaining only negative results, I substituted choke-cherries for the common or garden variety; and the pale horse still passed me by. "Three sunstrokes are sure death"; this saying I can neither corroborate nor refute; I got the first sunstroke, but never could get numbers two and three.

In a dramatic masterpiece called *Gay Paree*, a husband and wife were quarreling. "If you keep on like that," cries the male, "you'll drive me out of my mind." "Huh," retorts lovely woman, "that ain't a drive, that's a putt."

An irate farmer having captured a naughty lad who had been scaring his sheep, took the offender over his knee and was about to apply the palm of a large and powerful hand to the spot ordained by nature for such ministrations. "Hold on!" remonstrated a compassionate neighbor; "don't be too hard on that boy! He ain't quite all there." "Wal," rejoined the agriculturist, "I reckon there's enough of him there for my purpose."

Beholding a big tough pitch into a little one, in the slums, the excitable philanthropist steps up to the stalwart ruffian and thus delivers himself: "You are a great cowardly Irish bully!" "Will you say that again?" "You are a great cowardly Irish bully!" boldly repeats our Don Quixote. The brute scratches his head, looking down at his insulter. "Well, I can't help that," he at last replies bewildered-like. The only part of the rebuke that has penetrated his understanding is the word "Irish." The rest, I suppose, means no more than "tee um lie."

It is interesting to note how, in phrases that have become very familiar, the originally distinctive element has been eliminated: so "prohibition," "suffrage," "civil service." "I," said the politician, speaking perhaps more truly than he knew, "am an irreconcilable enemy to civil service." Similarly *opera* takes the place of "opera in musica," or "work in music"; *piccolo*, "little," means "piccolo flauto"; *piano*, "soft," signifies "pianoforte."

Have you ever tried to compute what propor-

tion of a discourse you need to understand, in order
to follow it all? From one-fifth to one-tenth of the
dialogue of a play will suffice, I believe — one-fifth
for a social satire, one-tenth for a melodrama. Of
course, under ordinary circumstances, we actually
hear only a small fraction of the sounds that are
discharged at us. These we patch together, filling
in the blanks, as in a cross-word puzzle. It must be
done with extreme rapidity, else we lose the thread.
Either in conversation or at the theatre, comprehension is as much a matter of the mind as of the
ear. And it is very largely a matter of habit; we
have in our heads an abundant assortment of
words, phrases, and intonations, and, given a scrap
of clue, can supply the rest. That is why a quick-
witted person, or an educated person, seems to hear
better than an illiterate or dull one. That is why,
too, it is so much harder to grasp a speech in a
foreign tongue. We really hear just as many of the
sounds as in our native vernacular, and our foreign
vocabulary may be just as adequate, but it is not
so readily available; before we have made good the
deficiencies in the first sentence, the second is under
way. You must have observed the phenomenon
known as "slow hearing." Somebody fires a sentence at you unexpectedly; you have not the least
idea what it is; but some minutes — even some
hours — later it may come to you. The key-
sounds have stuck in your memory and your men-

tal resourcefulness at last succeeds in completing the cross-word.

Sometimes you will be quite thrown off the track by a strange pronunciation of a single word. Two traveling companions of mine were quite at a loss when an English lady whose acquaintance we had made at a hotel in Pisa announced that she was "on her wy to Rowm and Nyples." At least, she had the look and manners of a lady. A cockney accent is often a complete barrier to comprehension, even though one be in theory quite familiar with its peculiarities.

How shall we pronounce queerly spelled place-names? I am told that in England there is now a tendency to speak them according to their orthography — to give Worcester, for instance, full credit for three syllables. With us, I should say, the theory is that the inhabitants of a place have the right to choose the style of its designation. So we say Arkinsaw, Mizzoora, and, if we know enough, Spoke Ann, Bill Ricker, and Will Lam It. Shall we go as far as I O Way, Sin Sin Atta, Chat Ham, and New Fun *Land*? In the case of technical terms, shall we follow the technicians or the dictionary? Shall it be *taycle* or *tackle*, *no'theast* or *northeast*? Must we imitate the physician when he mispronounces "cocaine," "trachea," "hygiene," and "paresis?"

That horrible last word awakens a sad reminiscence. He was a good, kind, elderly man, eccentric perhaps, but not inefficient, and he was principal of a city high school. One day he wanted to consult me very privately. We went into his office, and he carefully closed the door. "Have you noticed anything queer about me?" he whispered. "I've got paresis." "No," said I. "Although I have seen more or less of you for some years, I have never suspected anything of the kind. How does it show itself?" "It makes me silly with young women. I've got a lot of pretty girl pupils in the school, and I say soft things to 'em. You haven't observed it, perhaps, because I am still able to take care when there are people around. But I sometimes say spoony things; and, what's worse, I write spoony letters. I am sure some of these letters have come into the hands of parents, and they are going to make trouble for me. Of course it's paresis, because I never was like that before. If I could only stop writing letters, I'd be all right. Now, I want your advice. I don't care to lose my job; I'm good for several years yet. My idea is to write a letter to the School Board, telling 'em all about it, and explaining that I've got paresis. If I've got paresis, they can't blame me for it. I want 'em to hear about it from me before it come to 'em from anybody else. And I want 'em to know beforehand that it's paresis. If I tell 'em it's just paresis, they'll let me stay, don't you think so?" No, I

didn't think so. It was not long before the poor
man vanished from the scene.

I wonder whether mental disorder is commoner
among Anglo-Saxons than among other peoples.
At any rate, I am sure it is commoner in their
literature. In Germany and France, no doubt,
there have been quite as many crazy writers, but
not so many mad characters in fiction, even count-
ing in the epidemic of love-madness in the second
half of the eighteenth century. You all remember the
Lady Lunatic in *The Wizard of Oz*. Well, what a
theme for a dissertation would be the Lady Lunatic
in English literature! What figures rise out of the
grave! Ophelia, Lucy Ashton, Maria, the Woman
in White. Lucy, as everyone knows, has become an
operatic heroine. But not everyone knows (does
anyone know?) that Sterne's Maria also is identical
with the soprano of *Dinorah*, known in French as
Le Pardon de Ploërmel? Maria, you may remember,
is an incidental but very striking character both
in *Tristram Shandy* and in *A Sentimental Journey*.
A victim of disappointed love, she has gone gently
mad, and wanders about playing on a pipe and accompanied by a goat (which animal in the *Journey*
has been exchanged for a dog). Now, this is exactly the heroine of Meyerbeer's prettiest opera,
recently restored to favor by the singing of Galli-
Curci. The scene, as the French title suggests, is in

Britanny; and our Maria, goat, pipe, and all, is re-incarnated as Dinorah. It is one of those comfortable operas, like *The Magic Flute*, in which the book is so absurd that you don't have to worry about it, and the music can be as diversified and as lovely as you please. In fact, there is a beautiful chorus before the curtain goes up. Now, my question is: did the librettist get the figure from Sterne, or did both Sterne and the librettist draw from some real Breton story? The former seems to be more likely; yet Sterne must have got his Maria somewhere, for she is not the kind of person he would have been likely to invent. Here is a field for investigation. I have not even found out who wrote the text of *Dinorah*; it is hard to think Scribe composed anything so inane.

A mystic connection exists between complexion, voice, and character. I have noticed, by the way, that when a wife sings second bass, the husband is likely to be a light tenor. But what I had in mind was this: why is the hero always a tenor, and the villain a bass (or, at best, a baritone)? And why are the good people blond and the wicked brunette? This convention is so well established that we take it for granted. The golden-haired heroine and hero reach out beyond opera into poetry and romance; in fact, they are of very ancient extraction. Does their patent of nobility date back to the conquest of Mediterranean Greece by a Nordic race which set the aristocratic standard? Likely enough. But were the Nordic Hellenes all tenors? More research is needed in this quarter.

It is interesting to observe how conventions grow up on the stage. The blond and brunette standard goes back to classic times, or further; the tenor and bass rivalry comes down (with alterations) from the early days of opera. But some conventions have shaped themselves under our own eyes. Take the anvil chorus in *Il Trovatore*. One would think it needed no adventitious aid. But when electricity came into general use on the stage, some smart manager thought to enhance the effect by introducing sparks from contact of hammer and anvil. Presently these sparks became a necessary adjunct, increasing in brilliancy year by year, until, developing into a dazzling shower of Leonids, they have completely dwarfed both the song and the dramatic situation. Now the scene is an electric display set to music. Then there is the Chancellor's train-bearer in *Iolanthe* and the parasol-carrier in *The Mikado*. Incidentally introduced in one production, they have become regular personages. The train-bearer dates from the Chancellor of Henry Dixey, who wanted to bring his little boy on the stage and have a bit of sport with him. As to the parasol man, it is really only a few years since a supernumerary, inventing a graceful little dance step for that part, transformed it into a real rôle. The world knows how conspicuous those two mute personages became in the Winthrop Ames performances. I wonder how much (if any) of the technique of our playing of Shakspere goes back to similarly accidental origins.

We owe a debt to Shakspere for keeping alive the tradition of distinct and pleasurable utterance. Heaven only knows into what a chaos of brutish unintelligibility we might have sunk, without the stage. Much we owe to teachers of diction who train people for the theatre, and help to maintain a standard of some kind. One of the most intelligent, scientific, and forceful of these apostles was preparing, not so many years ago, a little volume of speech samples, showing the practice of variously located speakers, illustrated by passages in phonetic notation. For some reason, she — the apostle is a she, and a very charming one — wanted me as a local specimen. After several failures to make connection, she descended on Cambridge, expecting to run a pin through me; but I had already departed for the summer. In desperation she then called on President Eliot, who was still in town, and persuaded him to read aloud a page from one of my books. Whether he meant to give an imitation of me, I should greatly like to know, but have never been able to ascertain. She said he seemed immensely amused. The text does read just like me; but then, we spoke essentially the same dialect, being both of us Bostonians. So there, enshrined in her volume, my words are immortalized as rendered by Charles William Eliot — a model to such as, groping in phonetic darkness, allow themselves to be led to see the light.

BEHAVIOR

MOSES, my white tomcat, was very fond of me, and I was fond of him. I had done nothing whatever to displease him; therefore his remarkable behavior on that occasion cannot have been induced by resentment or hostility. No, he was the friendliest creature in the world. Often, when I would go down into the cellar of an evening, to attend to the furnace or to get an apple, he would sit on the end of one of the stairs, at the level of my head, and watch me with a look of affectionate interest. But he never could get used to apples. When I proceeded to eat one, his expression would change, first to curiosity, then to appetite, and he would lift his head, sometimes his paw, in supplication. At that, I would offer him a piece. One smell of it always convinced him that the thing was absolutely inedible. He would look from the apple to me, and from me to the apple, with a surprise that shaded into incredulity. When I took another bite, the process was repeated: same experiment, same amazement. After a few trials he would make up his mind either that I was juggling or that I was ruining my digestion. In either case he preferred not to witness the event; he would close — or half-close — his eyes and affect indifference; sometimes he even turned his back.

On the evening in question, however, there had been no such misunderstanding; my business had been solely with the furnace, which Moses comprehended and approved. My task completed, I was standing by the stairs conversing amicably with him, my face very close to his perch. Suddenly, without warning, he shuts his eyes, turns down his ears, and with his right forepaw makes a vicious dig at my left eyelid. I might have lost an eye. Fortunately, however, I pull back just in time and deal him a violent cuff on the left ear. Now, both his act and mine were certainly of the mechanical type known by the horrible name of behaviorism. Moses had no thought of doing me harm; for the instant, he was not aware that my eyelid was me. He saw something fluttering, and an urge outside his consciousness brought the inevitable reaction. We love to see a kitten play with a fluttering leaf. But play, with animals human and inhuman, consists usually in mitigated fighting; and that association accounts for the cat's closed eyes and flattened ears. For my part, I had no idea of evading or punishing. My head goes back as independently of my volition as an eye closes when a cinder flies at it; and my hand strikes as instinctively as it clutches when I am falling.

We are both of us behaviorists. As Keyserling would put it, the "animal" in us is uppermost.

Another example. I used to own a pair of fur gloves, which I wore on the coldest winter days. In all sorts of weather, as you know, dogs like to come up to a man, even a stranger, to be petted. This happened to me, over and over again, in the glove-wearing season. But a strange thing would ensue; whenever my gloved hand would approach the animal's nose, on its way to the top of his head, the creature, who hitherto had been all friendliness, would emit an ominous growl; one dog even snapped savagely at my hand. Evidently the scent of that fur aroused a hunting instinct so strong that it momentarily overpowered all sense of reality, and the dog acted like a machine.

In beasts and in men there are associations that go back to a previous stage of development, perhaps before the advent of reason; and if one of these primeval contacts is for a moment renewed with sufficient vigor, both beast and man return for that instant to the primeval state. Of course, the Behaviorists with a capital B would have us believe that all our acts, and the mental processes we choose to regard as thought, arise in this same mechanistic fashion; they would thus abolish will, and, with it, responsibility and morality. This doctrine I cannot bring myself to accept. Yet in our ordinary conduct I am daily impressed by the high proportion of mechanical or semi-mechanical movements due to hidden associations. And these associations need not be very ancient; they need not be inborn. For instance, the presence of salt and pepper in like receptacles on the dinner-table is not a hangover from pithecanthropic days; probably the coupling of them in our subconsciousness is achieved by each of us independently. Yet how many of us are able to pass the salt without at the same time passing the pepper? Try the experiment: ask for salt, and compute the number of times you get it bereft of its mate. I doubt whether even Rémy de Gourmont, the apostle of dissociation, could withstand the urge.

How mysteriously things are linked together, not only in our mental catalogue, but in bald reality! Here is an example. Along our beautiful Maine coast are sprinkled numerous establishments called "sardine factories," where "American sardines" are made from herring and cottonseed oil. There is no fraud about it; the boxes are accurately labeled. And the sardines are said to be fairly good. Now, immediately after the passage of the Eighteenth Amendment and the Volstead Act, this flourishing industry began to decline. In fact, it almost perished. Why? Had I been a Sherlock Holmes, I might have divined. Question one: have you ever seen American sardines on a dining-table? Question two: have you ever seen them

eaten anywhere? Question three: where? The
solution is now clear. The principal — almost the
only — market for the American sardines was the
American saloon, which purchased them for its
free-lunch table. That much is sure. But, these
things being so, how are we to account for the fact
that the industry has revived and is at present
busier than before? What are we to infer?

An interesting but often irritating association is
that of religion and politics. Very generally it is
assumed that in order to be a Socialist, or Com-
munist, or Nihilist, or whatever you may call it, a
man must be irreligious. Among the Russian Bol-
sheviks this notion has assumed the proportions of
a monomania. But even in comparatively sane
countries one finds the same idea. There is, to be
sure, a little-known party of Christian Socialists,
and the combination would seem to be as logical as
anything in politics can be; probably it is too logical
to be popular. I once had the privilege of dining
with M. Janvier, the Socialist mayor of the city of
Rennes. M. Janvier was originally a plasterer.
Possessing a talent for organization, he became
president of the Plasterers' Union in his town. At
this period he began to instruct himself in the arts
of reading and writing, and became a very effective
speaker. A political career was, as the French say,
"indicated." Step by step he rose to the chief
executive office, which he filled, year after year,

with competence and geniality. But for his un-
timely death, he probably would have reached the
national Senate. M. Janvier, then, was complain-
ing to me of the duplicity of mankind. "You think
you can put confidence in them, but all of a sudden
you find they have been deceiving you. It is almost
enough to make a man distrustful of every voter.
Why, here in Rennes there are forty thousand
people enrolled in the Socialist party; and I know
— I know for a fact — it seems too monstrous, but
it's true — that of these forty thousand at least
thirty thousand, as often as once a year, go to
church!"

A common man he was, in looks and in opinions,
though anything but common in ability. In the
eyes of his more polished compatriots, no doubt, he
was a vulgarian. We are often a bit surprised to
observe in different nations different standards of
vulgarity and elegance. Many a fellow-countryman have I met abroad, received as a gentleman,
who at home would have been outside the pale.
All too many others, be it said parenthetically,
bear the stamp of the noisy plebs wherever they
may go. Variations in speech make divers impressions according to our associations with them.
Slang differs from slang, error from error, by reason
of the habitual user. I dare say a Yankee in England may utter things which, though in his home
city they would write him down a bounder, may

pass on foreign soil as spicy Americanisms. Once, in Naples, I spent a week in the same *pension* with a middle-aged Englishman of attractive appearance — good clothes and quiet, affable manners — whom (I thought) his compatriots rather avoided, but whom I was glad to accept as a table-companion. He asked me whether, in Paris, I had attended any performances at the "Francus"; it took me some minutes to guess that he meant the Comédie française. Pompeii, he confessed, had been a sore disappointment to him; there was nothing to be seen but "hemty aouses." For me, that was just refreshingly foreign; in Boston, Mass., the vulgar use another line of vulgarisms.

Soon, no doubt, slang will be identical all over the world. The bad man from Butte will talk like the Tokio tough or the loafer in Liverpool. That is what the movies are for, and the radio. There is still, however, and will be (thank Heaven!) as long as I shall live, a shade of difference. It is so even with whiskers. In France big black beards are still prevalent; to an outsider they look odd, especially on youths in their early twenties. We used to think of Germany — next to Russia — as the land of bristly faces, but American razors plus American fashion seem to have done a good job of denudation. How many grades of facial hirsuteness we sexagenarians have witnessed in our time and country, from the majestically waving leg-of-mutton, or

Burnside, to the ultra-Charlie-Chaplin, which looks like an unwiped nose! We have even seen (occasionally) the paint-brush that decorates the symbolic chin of Uncle Sam.

Old Reuben Jay — so the story goes — used to sport that decoration, a marvelously long, stout, stiff hairy projection, which, starting from his lower jaw, proceeded downward and outward to an appalling distance. Imposing, slightly aggressive, it would have brought its wearer naught but honor, had it not been for infantile curiosity. "Grandpa," cried Willy, who in long silence had been studying the grandpaternal profile. "Grandpa!" "Well, my boy," wagged the whisker, "what is it?" "Grandpa, when you go to bed, do you tuck your beard inside the bedclothes, or outside?" "Gosh! I never thought of that," replied Reuben, "I just can't remember. But I'll try it tonight." And so he did. Ay me, ay me! First he thrust it under; but it pushed against the blankets like a spring, and seemed to lift them clean off his chest. Next he left it outside, and felt as if he were sleeping clothed beneath a tree. Under again! Intolerable pressure. Once more in the open! The wind went whistling through. Either procedure, when tried, seems unfamiliar. Shifting and shunting, turning and twisting, faster and still faster and furiouser, wondering and worrying, worrying and wondering, he at last worries himself into a congestion, and finds peace in death. And the question remains unanswered.

We really need no answer just at present, because paint-brushes are dead. But who knows how soon the whirligig of fashion may bring them around again? I expect hoop-skirts back within a decade. Several times in the decade past we have narrowly escaped them; and more than once in that time we have been threatened with a return of sideboards. Already we are getting other Victorian things which we thought forever buried: black walnut furniture with marble tops and horsehair seats, iron dogs and stags for the front yard. Such recurrences obey no conscious human desire: they must be manifestations of behaviorism.

What other power than behaviorism makes us all do the same things at the same time in the same way? Why else, at the moment of writing, do we all run and have our teeth pulled, whatever our malady? Shall our dentition follow the fate of the ladies' hair, only in the next decade to be painfully and slowly restored, as the ladies are regrowing their lost locks? I foresee the likelihood of a toothless period (doubtless a short one) for the devotees of style. "Let me tell you exactly what you need," solemnly opined the doctor; "your teeth must come out." "All right!" cried the patient, triumphantly lifting his new set from his mouth. "Here they are!"

Toothlessness, according to any absolute standard, is unsightly, and that is an argument in its favor, since behaviorism in this generation is running to the hideous, except in dwellings and in woman's attire — both of which, I predict, will soon join the general current. In poetry, in music, and in art there has been for some time a veritable cult of ugliness and obscurity. When I say "cult," it is my purpose to employ a word containing no suggestion of free will; for the whole thing is purely behavioristic. We all of us lift up our voices in praiseful unison when confronted with a roomful of watercolors supposed (I think) to represent the sea-shore, but looking like a cross between a kaleidoscope and a Russian ballet. For there is an involuntary, nay, a maniacal vogue of violent colors. Nature's hues, which are all soft and delicate half-tints, are turned into raw purples and crimsons. The music of the flute is translated into the language of the steam calliope. I suppose this latter instrument is appropriate in a society where all must be "leaders," since all have been "trained for leadership."

Not long ago, walking rapidly by an old book-shop, I caught from the corner of my eye a glimpse of a second-hand picture post-card, hanging in the window. "Why! that is an Opper!" I cried. "I never knew that he made picture-cards." And, sure enough, Opper it was, when I stopped to examine. The old shop had a series of them. You remember Opper, who used to draw caricatures for *Puck* — scenes drawn from the ordinary, but drawn (with very little exaggeration, and a minimum of mannerism) in a style so far from the ordinary as to be recognizable at a half-look forty years after. Again, only a few weeks since, I was sitting in the waiting-room of the Grand Central; away across the hall a man unfolded a newspaper, in which I instantly recognized a small-scale reproduction of one of Thomas Nast's cartoons. Apparently, before everyone was trained for leadership, some people had a chance to be different from others.

I was a boy once, with a boy's enthusiasm; and for a time I was daft over wood-engraving, even to the extent of longing to cut pictures, myself, on the block. Guidance I sought, but it was hard to find. Everybody, with smiling and sympathetic benevolence, directed me to somebody else. Teachers, artists, printers all handed me along the line. At last I was told of two brothers, successful cartoonists, who could tell me if anyone could. They had a little office somewhere down-town; thither I tremblingly betook myself, and found the pair busily at work, turning out cartoons to order. They kindly listened, though, to my story, and even stopped a moment to think of something helpful to say. To be sure, they could not think of much; but I found compensation in watching them and their rapidly growing pictures. "You must be very happy," I exclaimed, after a while. "To think of having such a business as this! Don't you enjoy every minute of it?" They both stopped abruptly, and stared at me. Then one, with a wistful look, replied, resuming his task as he spoke: "I can remember a time, now that you speak of it, when I did get a lot of pleasure from every picture I made — just from doing it, you understand. Now, when I am drawing a cartoon, all I can think of is how much money I shall get for it." They were not too case-hardened, however, to appreciate the creations of others; and Nast, the master of the craft, was their especial deity — not perfect, but supreme. "Nast never could draw a woman," said the less taciturn brother (and subsequent study has corroborated his startling statement), "but, my God! how he could draw men!"

This is no time for an Opper or a Nast. It is the age of behaviorism.

CRACKS IN THE CLOUDS

It gives you a strange intoxication to spend a night on a mountain. Not the bracing air alone — there is also the consciousness of being above the world, in another sphere of existence; and a peculiar lightness, both of foot and of head. It is something like your experience in dreams, when you overcome gravity and float off into space or bob up against the ceiling. When I was twelve, I remember, I slept on the Righi, after having walked up. Later I had a night on the Gorner Grat, amidst the snow peaks. Moosilauke was not so pleasant, because it rained furiously and my sheets were damp; wet sheets do dampen one's enthusiasm. But good old Mt. Washington, the top of New England! Many's the night I have spent there, in the old Tip Top House or the big Summit House. When I say "many," I suppose I mean about eight. Anyhow, I once put in a three days' stay there, with grand, sunny excursions above the timber line, visiting the spots I had never had time to turn out for, on the climb up or down.

That sojourn followed a wearisome ascent in a snowstorm. We had lodged in a dilapidated house at the foot, called Darby Field Cottage, to be ready for an early start up through Tuckerman's Ravine. The evening was fair, but not without premonition of trouble. There were three of us, Carl, Max, and I, on an extended tramp through the mountains. I think it was in October. In the Darby Field Cottage there were two chambers available. Carl and Max drew the spacious one, with several articles of furniture, whilst I got a tiny hall bedroom, with nothing but a cot bed. They laughed at me as we said "good-night"; but ere morn the laugh was transferred to the other side of their mouths. For my ceiling was sound, whereas their roof had a great hole directly over the bed, and it snowed hard in the night.

The snow continued in the morning, but we decided, with easy optimism, that it would "soon clear up." It didn't. The sun dimly penetrated the clouds for an hour or two, and then went out. And the snow went on, while a solid mass of mist came rolling up the ravine. By the time we had reached the head, above the Snow Arch, one couldn't see fifty feet; it was sleeting pitilessly, and a treacherous blanket of snow covered over the mile of broken rock which lay between us and the summit. There was nothing to indicate direction except Carl's compass and my recollection of the topography, both of which Max profoundly distrusted. A shivery consultation, with the help of a map, resulted in a painful retreat to the lower part of the ravine, where a trail ran across to the carriage road.

"Ran" is doubtless too rapid a word. The trail was there, according to specifications, and we eventually found it; but it did not run, it crawled. Indeed, so slow was its slippery serpentine course that the afternoon was far spent and it was nearly pitch dark when we struck the road. A light greeted us: the ever welcome Half-Way House, where some hot tea restored our desire to live. Four miles more in the face of a boreal blast, under pelting sleet, up a road that was easy in grade but so smoothly coated with ice that we slipped back two steps out of every three. After a blank eternity, something dim and dark seems to loom up suddenly beside us. The old Summit House stable! I recognize it. But Carl by this time is impervious to any ray of hope. Max does not believe, but has the will to do so. "You two go on, if you can," declares the fatalistic Carl, "I am going to sit right here, with my back to the wall, and wait for daylight." Vain were persuasion and exhortation. If there were such a thing as the top (which he doubted), the morrow might reveal it. Down he sat, the picture of desperate determination; and there he would have sat until the crack of doom, if two great bloodhounds, sent out from the hotel, had not come sniffing and barking at us. Reluctantly convinced that we were only a few steps removed from life, light, and warmth, Carl rose to his feet, and all three of us, with our canine escort, stiffly staggered up to the platform.

What a sight we must have been! From the ends of Carl's drooping mustache hung two long icicles, giving him the appearance of a walrus. I rather favored a polar bear; my thin clothes, having been soaked through and through and then frozen stiff as cardboard, were coated with white frost, as were my cap and hair. Max wore a hat which had been a bowler, fastened on with a handkerchief tied over the top and under his chin. Yet nobody laughed. Nothing but angelic solicitude. It was a heavenly refuge. A bath, a hard rub, a good dinner turned us into living human things again. We even played ping pong that evening. I could hear other people playing it, I thought, all night. The most nerve-racking of games.

The next morning was bright, and by ten all the snow had vanished. Of those following three days I need say nothing further. When the time came for departure, we once more, of one accord, laid our course for the bar, to offer the final libation. "Going?" said the dispenser of beverages — a humorist by nature, and glad, on that mountain-top, to find an appreciative listener. "Well, I'm sorry. You boys have been good customers. And you've behaved fine. You ain't raised no row, and you ain't tried to flirt with the table girls. Come back soon!

This drink is on the house." And he even consented (contrary to rules) to join us.

But I had intended to feature a sunrise; all that precedes has been circuitously leading up to it. Seeing the sun come up is a part of the Summit House ceremonial. The orb emerges to the accompaniment of a gong — and very early, at an hour when the thermometer is in the depths. Guests are warned, by a placard in every chamber, not to take their bed blankets out of doors with them. The spectacle is well worth a shiver; and after it one can scuttle back into a warm bed, if one has remembered the number of one's room and has not forgotten the key. Well, one morning, as we stepped forth on the platform, we found ourselves on a little island. Right about us was the top of the mountain; above us, the clear heaven, wherein some bold stars had not yet yielded to the light that was spreading from a red horizon; below our islet, as far as the eye could reach in every direction, an undulating expanse of white, an unbroken sea of cloud. The earth had sunk away beneath the opaque ocean, and we were alone with the sky. As the sun climbed, from time to time the white floor would split open, just a crack, and for a moment we had a glimpse of a tiny slice of that lost world, until the rift closed again. In great clearness and brightness we could see it, but only for an instant. And the breaks were not always in the same spots; here and there they shifted, allowing inspection of this bit and that of the hidden land. Finally, of course, the huge surface broke up and disappeared, with amazing swiftness, and the whole world was spread out at our feet, the valleys still full of mist, the uplands glaring in the sunshine. Then from the low places the mists would come curling upward, joining forces and threatening to isolate us once more; but they were no match for the sun; they would either fade into nothingness or roll off on high as fleecy clouds.

One may well imagine, if so disposed, that in some future existence the curtain that separates us from our past will roll away, and all will be clear to us. Meanwhile, however, in the life we know, we catch only transient glimpses through rifts in the screen. Why the veil of forgetfulness should break here and not there, now and not then, we cannot tell. Some flitting association, I suppose, opens a momentary circuit connecting present and bygone. The pictures come unbidden, always a surprise, usually a delectation.

Frequently, in summertime, I have for a moment the illusion of lying in a field of tall grass — monumentally tall, shielding and shading me as I lie. Quite cut off from contact with humankind, I enjoy membership in a larger and older society, the ancient and honorable society of insects, which thickly peoples that forest. How interesting all their operations are, when viewed from the appropriate distance of six inches! Grasshoppers are my favorites, with their extraordinary combination of sedateness and agility. Have you ever noticed how they perform an about-face during a jump? I love to hold them gently just before they spring, and feel in my hand the tremendous push of those powerful hindlegs. And how wise they look as they sit and chew tobacco! The only disadvantage of intimacy with this world of Lilliput is that the friendships you form are so one-sided: in the consciousness of these little beings, you are just a part of the landscape, an earthquake if you move, a harmless hummock if you are still; but you must try to forget that. For you are at a time of life when all your interest is in individuals. Each tree, each bush, each plant that you know has its own self, its own character; so it is with those savages who have no word for the species but give different names to the different specimens that surround them. And you hate to believe that you have no distinctness in the eyes of creatures who are so distinct in yours.

Little things delight the little. I can see a tiny, tiny house right beside a railway track. When I visit there, I have the feeling of a toy house built for me. I must be about five, I fancy. The occupants are a small pair (although Mr. J. B. is growing a tummy), and they have no children. There are just enough rooms, and each room is just big enough to hold the requisite furniture. The windows are beautiful with shades displaying romantic castles in dark brown. The shades, of course, have to be small, to fit the windows, so the castles can not be very big. Whenever a train goes by, the whole house shakes like jelly, and the shades flap with a joyous noise. The yard is just extensive enough to surround the house and a diminutive stable. It always seems to me that this latter edifice must have been constructed over and around the horse and the buggy, while these inmates stood still for the operation; otherwise such a snug fit is hardly conceivable. Overhead is a loft with a capacity of one portion of hay. The horse is rather an undersized animal, excepting his feet, which call for considerable floor-space. Judging from the situation of his home, I think Mr. J. B. must at this moment have some connection with the railway, but I am not sure. He has had so many professions! Blacksmith, fireman, policeman, carpenter, cook, peddler — have you ever heard of so versatile a genius? Good in all these callings; yet, I fear, with no consecutive fondness for any. The last trade, perhaps, best suits his disposition, for he has a cheery temper, with a copious current of conversation, and an aptitude for sitting in a cart behind a horse. Some pleasant memories of his earlier pursuits he must cherish, for he still from

time to time exercises the functions of carpenter
and cook, and officiates as special policeman. His
badge, big and shiny (the one big thing in his little
house), is to me, and to him, a thing of wonderment. He is most fully himself at the season of the
County Fair, when he performs the double duty of
guarding the peace and fabricating his justly
famous chowder. Not infrequently he is invited to
furnish this delicacy at municipal banquets and
church sociables. Once he took me to a sociable
at the opening of a new church — Baptist, I am
pretty sure. I remember benches, bread and butter, dishes, all of which had to be contributed by
various well-wishers, and immense quantities of
chowder. Mr. J. B. is all aglow with benevolent
bustle and self-satisfaction, his very tummy seems
to swell; and I am proud (God forgive me!) to be
the guest of so important a personage. One more
characteristic of Mr. J. B. deserves mention. He
has a mania for swapping things. I have known
him thus to acquire a brass watch chain, a thick
silver watch that would go while you watched it
(these two, however, he did not possess simultaneously), a pistol with a barrel two feet long,
which you had to hold with both hands. I always
suspected that he had come by his horse in similar
fashion. By the same process of exchange or bar-
ter, and at his suggestion, I procured from him, by
sacrifice of a jackknife with which I had just cut

my finger, an old opera glass, long the envy of my playmates. It had all its lenses, but they were loose and rattled around inside it. If you contrived to shake them into the right positions you could see through it, darkly; but you had to manage it like a kaleidoscope.

The kaleidoscope shifts, and another picture comes to view. I am sitting on a hassock in our living-room, and my mother and a female cousin of hers are singing together. I must be very young indeed, for it is my first perception of counterpoint. No such word is in my vocabulary, and I have no idea what it is. Merely the magic of two voices together, it seems to me. But it thrills me through and through. Fine counterpoint still affects me in the same way. For most non-musical people, I fancy, the melody is the more important thing, but not for me. A tune is something to be caught and remembered; while counterpoint, mysterious and elusive, recalled only without volition, in dreamlike flashes, is the thing that seems to transmute the listener.

Another sudden transition. This is the dear old Boston Museum, for many, many years our most cherished playhouse. I mean the museum of William Warren, Mrs. Vincent, Annie Clarke, and Charles Barron, long before the days of Mason, Haworth, Sadie Martinot, and George Wilson of beloved memory. My mother used to take me there as early as I was able to sit in a seat; and in after life, whenever I got a chance, there I would sit, until its demolition. So innocent was I in my first phase that when Miss Annie Clarke's deep voice proclaimed, in the last act of *Lady Audley's Secret*, "I am mad — that is me long-kept and well-kept secret," I wondered what she had to be mad about; several of the other characters seemed to me to have much more serious grievances. Well, in those days (I wonder how many theatre-goers remember it), a part of the proscenium decoration consisted of a tall, upright, narrow mirror on each side of the stage, erected at such an angle that I could see in it the reflection of a small segment of the spectators. It was like looking at the public through a crack. How it did puzzle me! Again and again I would ask my mother where "that other audience" was; but I never could make her understand. Apparently, indeed, there were three distinct audiences, although I never could see more than two at a time; and they were all watching the stage from different quarters. After the play, while in the crowd we were slowly making our way out, I would peer eagerly around in a never-ending and never-satisfied endeavor to locate those other two halls. The building was a big one, surely; but the space outside our own familiar auditorium appeared to be all taken up with the biological and ethnological collections — not to speak of the dusty waxworks in the top story. The architectural problem was never solved: ere I reached an age when I might have worked it out, the looking-glasses were removed.

After the demise of the Museum, the Tremont Theatre was long my favorite. I liked the pieces given there, I liked the tasteful decorations, and I liked the old habit (preserved for a number of years after the other houses had given it up) of selling the good seats, as well as the bad, at the box office. Listen to this. One day I was calling at a shop — a little shop away upstairs on a side street — the shop of an elderly Swiss watchmaker, an excellent workman of the old school, so tall that he never seemed to have quite room to stand up straight in his restricted quarters. As I entered, he was conversing with a friend, perhaps a fellow-countryman; and while I was discussing my watch's symptoms with the practitioner, I could not help noticing that this stranger kept observing me secretly and curiously. My business ended, I was about to go, when he addressed me. "I must beg your pardon, sir, for staring at you; it is because your face is so familiar to me. You doubtless have never seen me, but I have seen you a thousand times. You always have a seat near me; and I like to watch you because you seem to enjoy the show so much. I am the leader of the orchestra in the Tremont Theatre."

Once, indeed, I did accomplish three operas in two days, a Friday and a Saturday; which is pretty good for a non-professional. But that was in New York, at the Metropolitan. After the third, finding myself in no mood for bed, I walked down to the *Sun* office, where I knew a member of the night staff; and after the edition had been made up, he and I and a colleague of his, called "the Deacon," repaired to the "Prescription Room" of a neighboring pharmacy. Before our conclave parted, the affairs of the nation had been settled. Ah me! the days of long ago!

But the clouds are splitting again, and my next look takes me into a real remoteness. I see myself quietly waiting to be called for, in the establishment of a redistributor of capillary covering. No, not a red Indian, but a very Nordic gentleman, who with his son carries on a lucrative and highly confidential business. "B. F. B. & Son, Dealers in Human Hair," on West Street; a candy shop is there now. I am not in that emporium for commercial reasons, being in no need of additional locks and not caring to part with any that I have. Simply, B. F. B. is a friend of the family and my parents sometimes let me visit him for a bit, while they make a call. A rather extensive front portion of the shop is accorded to hirsute displays; and wonderful fabrications they are, including the widely advertised "B. F. B. Part," which looks so natural that nobody can tell it from reality. In this impressive *milieu* strangers are received; here, in low tones full of sibilants, their needs are set forth and satisfied. But the secret consultation room, for regular customers, is upstairs. Of course I am never admitted to that sanctuary, but I have several times succeeded in seeing the door opened or closed by a mysteriously smiling attendant. Immediately behind the showcase region, the main room is laterally bisected by a screen, such as one often sees in churches. Indeed, the whole atmosphere of the place is ecclesiastic; people walk about on tiptoe and converse in whispers; one breathes an incense of sympathetic discreetness. Behind the rood screen I am not permitted to look, but I know that sundry young ladies are seated in this choir, engaged in making things of which one never speaks aloud: wigs, fronts, switches, chignons, detachable curls. I know, because the door has to be partly opened from time to time; besides, if I sit near the screen, I can hear them softly talking and laughing together. There can be no doubt, then, about their existence; although it never enters my fancy that they can exist otherwise than as a function of the shop. That they should indulge in laughter, even of the most subdued type, rather shocks my sense of propriety.

The real charm of the spot, for me, lies not so much in its mystery and its delightfully creepy semi-silence, its absence of the bustle and ostentation of ordinary life, as in the presence of great files of *Harper's Weekly*, with which I am invited to amuse myself. I need no encouragement. An exhaustless store of excitement is that pile of back numbers, distinguished from the pale present by the cartoons of Thomas Nast. Was there ever any thing in black and white so colorful, so unerringly bold, so full of life? Ulysses S. Grant was Nast's hero, as he was mine. There was the Tweed Ring, all of whose members I learned to know so well. I suppose the credit for its downfall belongs chiefly to the great caricaturist. It is odd, by the way, that our two greatest political cartoonists should have been Germans: Nast and Keppler — Keppler of *Puck*, author of the "Tattooed Man," which contributed so much to the defeat of Blaine.

The picture which the cloud-rifts oftenest exhibit represents me in a big chair, reading. Always in a formidable library. It is my father's, for he was a reckless and miscellaneous collector of books. He collected them, however, not for the sake of collecting, but to read. And read them he did — a veritable Comestor! So catholic was his taste that *nil humani* (or next to nothing) was absent. A pretty full set of the Latin Classics in old calf-bound volumes. The German Romanticists in all sorts of make-up: two complete editions of Tieck, I remember, and two of Hoffmann. All Beyle and all Voltaire. Strauss's *Life of Jesus*, Locke, Comte, Thiers; Abbott's *Life of Napoleon*, with its illustrations on nearly every page, the hero always portrayed in flawless skin-tight breeches. The English Classics from Shakspere down. American humorists, caricaturists, actors, and poets. Who now remembers Sam Slick, Major Jones, Sol Smith, John Phoenix, Squibob? Astronomy, physics, and exploration, as most recently set forth. A long line of mathematics. A special alcove (so to speak) of Semitic: the *Thousand and One Nights* in several Arabic editions, and translations in various languages. Grammars and dictionaries galore; Lemprière's *Classical Dictionary*, so eagerly studied by Keats. Among all these, surely, there were some rarities, valuable even from the mercantile point of view; but my father would have lost his temper had anyone offered to buy. Then, a great mass of nondescript products of the press, nearly all of them interesting in one way or another. For instance an anonymous volume entitled *A Gentleman in Black; and Tales of Other Days*, illustrated by Cruikshank, which I ultimately found to be the work of Washington Irving.

I recall one novel described by my father as "the crudest book he had ever read," which, when the library came into my hands, I destroyed because it so disgusted me. I wish I had it now, for I have never seen or heard of another copy. It was written before our Civil War by a Southerner, a Judge Somebody-or-Other, a rabid anti-abolitionist; its title was *Spiritual Vampirism, or the Life* (or *Adventures* or something like that) *of Ethereal Softdown*. Ethereal Softdown was the fiendish protagonist. Having started as an ugly, feeble, stupid creature, she would captivate desirable men, one by one, and suck the wits and strength and beauty out of them, leaving them poor wrecks, while acquiring satanic charm for herself. How she got and married her first victim, "a comely young Quaker," is left untold. Even at the end, she is no Helen of Troy, for she still betrays, at critical moments, an "obliquity of the left eye"; and she is compelled to resort to the pretense of having accidentally torn the sleeve out of her dress in order to assure a conquest by displaying her bare arm. You see how the story dates. The climax comes in a contest between this siren and a young Southern gentleman who has ventured into New York, that cesspool of sin. The hero shares and voices his author's views on the race question. Standing at night amid the interminable, monotonous streets of the great city, gazing up at the endless lines of dark houses, he sees from time to time a mysterious light flash dimly from this window or that, and says to himself that probably in all these buildings miscegenation is now in process. How the tale ends, I have forgotten.

As to Irving's *Gentleman in Black*, that is a devil story. Two fashionable young men, one in England, one in France, near the close of the eighteenth century, bargain with the Evil One, disguised as a respectable gentleman in sombre garb, who grants limitless wealth in exchange for the performance of a stated amount of sin, which multiplies from year to year, like war debts. His Highness is eventually worsted by an elderly English lawyer, who takes the case in hand. That part is interesting, and so are the opening scenes; the rest is pretty tedious. It is a pity, by the way, that the victims could not have seen Cruikshank's pictures in advance; then they would never have mistaken the identity of their murky visitor.

The Arabic books, with their pretty but undecipherable type, were a lure. And my father's enthusiasm for the *Arabian Nights* was an incentive. When I was thirteen or so, therefore, I set out to learn Arabic. I had a little pamphlet grammar of modern Arabic and an eighteenth-century folio Arabic-Latin dictionary. Progress was slow, for several reasons. The words in the lexicon being arranged by roots, one had to guess the root of one's word before looking it up. Even then sometimes it was not there. And sometimes, when it was there, the Latin definition stumped me. I am proud to remember that I persevered in spite of

these difficulties, and eventually succeeded in reading a page or two.

One day my father gave me a surprise. I must
have been about eleven. We were rummaging
about in the garret, when in a forgotten corner we
came across a tall heap of uniform pamphlets tied
together. This package he pulled out, dusted, ex-
amined, and then turned over to me with the remark that perhaps it would interest me, since I was
fond of reading. O joy! The pamphlets were no
other than Beadle's Dime Novels! I lost no time;
seated there in the attic, I greedily began the first.
The second was traversed at second speed. The
third began to pall a bit. And I stuck fast in the
fourth. I have never had the courage to try one
since. But the gift was put to good use; carrying
my stock to school, I started a Beadle Loan Library among my mates; and, although I exacted no
payment, I won considerable regard. I have often
wondered what was my father's motive in bestow-
ing on me that heap of sensational literature. Did
he simply think it would amuse me, as it had
doubtless amused him for a moment? Or did he
believe that it would so cloy as to cure me of hunger
for cheap stuff? At any rate, it did; and he was
wise enough to foresee it.

School. I am in the Roxbury Latin School, to
which I have recently been transferred from a

public grammar school where I served my apprenticeship. A pretty thorough training it has been, especially in arithmetic, grammar, and reading aloud. This last exercise is now under way, in the scene that returns to me. A Trustee of the School, dear old Mr. Dillaway, is visiting the class. He merits, if anyone ever did, the title of "gentleman of the old school." After listening with an indulgent smile to the efforts of my mates, he observes me (I notice) with peculiar attention; and when I have done my bit, he speaks, in his soft, deliberate voice. "I like this boy's reading," he says, "because he seems to be the only one who has been correctly taught. I mean, taught as I was taught when I was a boy. He holds the book in his left hand, at the height of his elbow, with his thumb and little finger above and the other three fingers below the volume. And he holds his feet at an angle of forty-five degrees." Dear me! what has become of that angle in this cubistic age? But it certainly was drilled into us in the grammar school. Another critical angle was that at which the pen should be held in writing. The forearm must rest lightly on the elbow and the end of the little finger; and the pen, held between the thumb-tip and the first joint of the forefinger, must point over the right shoulder. One teacher, to be sure, held for the right eye, but her doctrine was finally declared unorthodox. Does anyone ever write in that fashion after escaping from bondage? While in the galley, of course, one bends to the oar. There was a special writing-expert who would inspect the school at frequent intervals. I can see him walking slowly up and down the aisles, glaring at the cramped little hands. Once in a while he stops, and, pointing across the room, begins to jump up and down, shrieking: "There's a boy holding his pen the wrong way!" Old age has its compensations: it can hold its pen as it likes, and can still get pleasure from holding it wrong. I never could write a decent hand until I did.

The mention of old people opens another rift, and I find myself in Cummington, a pretty village in western Massachusetts. It has a plenty of aged folk, to be called on whenever we visit my uncle and aunt there. You see, my mother used to live in Cummington when she was a girl; she was born in the neighboring village of Goshen. Her name was Lucretia; and as long as any of the eldest generation survived, I was in that community nothing but Crishy's Boy. Never could I understand why these decrepit and toothless men and women, so gentle and apparently so near the grave, should want to see me; but they did, there could be no doubt about it. They would have been hurt if I had not come; and when I did appear they would pat my head and say how I had grown. What on earth could they see in me? I saw nothing of interest in them, but I tried to be dutifully decent; and I hope I was just a bit touched. Old Mrs. Bigelow was somewhat different. She lived all alone in a wee house that was a regular curiosity shop — Malay clubs, Chinese teapots, Indian lacquer, a baby crocodile (stuffed). I fancy Mr. Bigelow — for there must have been one, in the inconceivable past — was a sea-captain. She was very kind, and ready to tell stories about her treasures. But one had to remember to ask her about her rheumatism. Each of these old people had some special infirmity that must be made a subject of inquiry, and that was something of a nuisance, especially as the answers were never very encouraging. They would talk rather freely about me, too. The general verdict was that I was destined to have a Burgess nose and a Burgess stomach, both of which seemed to be highly undesirable possessions. In fact, my boyhood was passed under a dark cloud of apprehension. When at last I reached the age of twenty without developing a Burgess nose (a very good nose, though, if I do say so) it began to dawn upon me that I might thwart heredity with regard to the stomach also. Since then my digestion has been perfect — unless I eat garlic or cucumbers.

It struck me as very strange that my uncle and aunt had no children. They were just the sort who ought to have some, they were so good to me. But my mother warned me that I must never, never mention the subject to them. Then the wonderment was all the greater, until one day I discovered a little grave in the cemetery behind the Baptist Church; and I understood.

My uncle had Billy, though, a spirited old horse who was kept like a spoiled boy. It was great fun to see him roll in the grass and kick his legs in the air, when uncle took him out to play in the evening. He had a stall four times as big as the ordinary, and lots of choice food; and a good time when hitched to the buggy, too, for he was a sport and my uncle was a fast and fearless driver. One had to be careful, because Billy, despite his excellences, was inclined to bite and kick. Like so many biters and kickers, he lived to a very ripe age; before he died, he had turned snow-white.

Uncle Franklin was a portly, courteous, dignified man, sometimes stern but habitually jolly — at least with my parents and me. He kept the village store, and sang bass in the church choir. When politics were propitious, he had the post office. Once a year, to lay in stock, he would make a pilgrimage to the city; and on those occasions we had the satisfaction of entertaining him in Boston. Really, he did not then appear particularly countrified, except his hair-cut.

I still love the composite smell of a country store, and I still love the sight of rolls of cloth in proximity to suspended scythes. It made life so simple.

Customers were not expected to come at meal-times. If they (strangers, I suppose) were so indiscreet, they were authoritatively but politely told to wait until dinner should be over; and wait they did, although uncle never hurried. The most anxious person, on such occasions, seemed to be myself, who, not daring to leave my seat, would eagerly attempt, every time the dining-room door was opened, to peep into the adjacent store, to see whether the customers were manifesting impatience. Had they departed, we should have heard their boots, for the new refectory, where we sat, was but thinly separated from the older building. This original structure contained, above the store, a choice bedroom, a library in which were to be found fascinating township maps of the county on a generous scale, and a broad, rather formal parlor opening on an upper piazza. For restful detachment and watchful privacy, there is nothing like an upper piazza — unless it be a mountain-top. There one may sit on a Sunday afternoon, when playing is tabu.

Play, of course, is pleasurable beyond aught else, but pleasure is sometimes a pain. For instance, when you are allowed to go barefoot. It was my vaulting ambition to walk unshod, like the village boys; and from time to time my mother yielded, with warnings against stone-bruises. If the angels fell by ambition, they can hardly have suffered from that sin more than I. Have you ever, unprotected, run across a new-mown field? There was one such, conveniently opposite, running down to the river. I can feel the prick of that pitiless stubble even now. How good was the sensation of cool water, after an experience like that! There was one particular deep spot, below the old dam, with a flat rock beside it. The water was over one's knees, and minnows would come and nibble at one's legs. But one could fish there all day without catching so much as a cold.

It was not there that I learned to swim; both incentive and water supply were insufficient. It was on a bend of the Blackstone River, not far from the Blackstone railway station, that I found sufficiency of both. There, under a great maple, whose branches spread far over the current, was the old hole which swimmers frequented, and in their company the aspiring neophytes. The art came to me in a flash. I was in the habit of clinging to a maple branch and, thus sustained, venturing considerably beyond my depth. Suddenly, one fine day, the envious sliver broke, and I was precipitated upon my own resources. These proving to be unexpectedly adequate, fear fled, never to return. After that, no body of water was so large or so small as to avoid invasion. There was a little pond in Jamaica Plain, near the Brookline border, where some of us used to practise the art. Though surrounded by bushes and trees, it was close to the high road, and one had to look out for the police. Now, indeed, it is included in the parkway. More than once we were warned off, but once only were we pursued. When that burly officer made a dash at us, the only thing we could do was to seize our clothes in our arms and plunge through the bushes. We should not have minded it so much, had they not been blackberry bushes, very thick and very sharp. I dare say the worthy cop was as relieved at our escape as we were.

Blackberries Cummington certainly had, and raspberries, such as have never grown elsewhere since the "garden eastward in Eden" — along the roads, in fantastic abundance, and up over the hills. And chokecherries down by the river. If you pushed on up the hillside through the sweet fern, you came to a wood and a brook — the Bryant place. In that old house the poet lived as a boy, and beside that brook he wrote *Thanatopsis*. He came to be Cummington's patron saint. I saw him once, a stately figure, with druidical white hair and beard; and I shall always regret that I could not be present at the consecration of his home on a recent summer.

My statement about blackberries needs qualification, for I remember Brittany — especially the Côtes du Nord, which I know best. No garden can surpass that country for copiousness of *mûres* and the thorny *ronces* on which they grow. They are coarser than ours, and perhaps not so good; at any rate, the people never eat them raw, for fear of colic. But the bushes do sprawl over the wayside, obstructive as the *ajoncs*, or gorse, hedges of which, perched on dikes, separate one little square lot from another. The gorse supplies most of the fuel, too, for it grows very big; it has no leaves — only thorns and flowers. A fairy realm, with its ultramarine sea, its sandy beaches parted by great rocky promontories, its daily showers, its balmy air, its hills sprinkled with picturesque stone cottages. Picturesque, and delightfully unsanitary, with no windows to windward; the older ones have thatch roofs and dirt floors, and many can still show those coffin-like air-tight bunks to sleep in. Above the cabin towers the manure heap, the owner's pride; and just beside this majestic pile is the well. No wonder the Bretons are a melancholy folk, and no wonder they die off like flies. The children, though, are pretty as pictures. And when I say "pictures," you know what kind of pictures I do not mean.

No bit of that world can be dissociated from my friend Georges, with whom I tramped it all, and with whom I shall never tramp it again. The old castle of Coatfrec, amid the beeches, with a sabot-maker's temporary shelter near by; the great ruin of Tonquédec, a stronghold destroyed by Richelieu, now buried in the forest; the hill of Ménébré, crowned by a village; the walled mediaeval town of Moncontour (the one near St. Brieuc), just at the border where the inhabitants begin to speak French. In the Côtes du Nord, many of the country-folk do not even understand it, except a few phrases. And the French of Moncontour would be hard to understand in Paris; for instance, I remember hearing for *suivre*, "follow," the strange word *sieudre*. Ancient chapels galore, housing grotesque little wooden saints; one old church with its columns all askew. "Ancient" and "old" mean little here; for everything is ancient in popular repute, and, thanks to the moist wind, everything made ten years ago looks centuries old. And the styles do not change. Only this: the insurance companies insist on slate roofs, instead of thatch.

Most unreal are the rocks on the shore (a reminder of the Franklin's Tale) and the intervening stretches of fine, hard sand. Trégastel exhibits a collection of extravagant stone shapes that pass belief. They actually exist, though, and are the work of nature — not like that other beach (what is its name?) where a primitive artist carves great human forms in the living rock. Scarcely less distinctive are the towns. Lannion, with its slate façades and its out-of-door palms; Perros-Guirec, and the quaint microscopic episcopal city of Tréguier, both of them immortalized by Renan; Paimpol, which Pierre Loti endowed with a star in the guide-book; Pènevenant, that village reverently called "le bourg" by the dwellers in still smaller hamlets round about; Plougrescant, opposite the island where the composer Thomas made his home; Plouguiel — it is astonishing how many of these Breton names begin with P!

All this I visited with Georges, for we were both good walkers. I first knew him in Paris, where we were fellow-students of Celtic, nearly half a century ago, and we kept up our friendship to the end. He achieved international distinction in science and local importance in politics. His career would be interesting to relate; but there is only one incident — an odd one — that I am going to tell. He and his wife had taken to themselves a little girl, having lost, to their acute sorrow, a daughter of their own. They had two older sons. A shy little thing when I first knew her, the wee stranger grew up a fine girl, a comfort to the family. So dear did she become that Georges and his wife forgot she was not of their blood, until some premonition of impending fate reminded them that Jeanne was not even a legally adopted child. I believe one of her real parents was still alive, and under those circumstances she could not become absolutely the daughter of another. At any rate, the law offered some impediment. Georges, then, was compelled to consider what was to become of her if he should die; for she could not share in his inheritance and he did not wish to leave her a dependent. To be sure, she was being trained for a profession; but it was a ladylike and poorly compensated one, and very precarious. In this emergency he asked his oldest son to marry her. This the lad indignantly refused to do, declaring that such a union would seem to him like incest, since they had grown up as brother and sister. Next, in desperation, Georges hit upon the idea of claiming Jeanne as a daughter of his own, born out of wedlock. Fortunately he consulted a lawyer, who told him to his consternation that such an act would be perjury, subject to extremely severe penalty if discovered (as it was pretty sure to be). Nevertheless, he would have persisted, had not his legal friend forbidden it, with threat of exposure; so he was compelled to make such provision as he could in his lifetime. Could this have happened anywhere else?

It is hard to tear one's self away from the seashore, however contrary to one's prejudices that shore may be. Could you, O Bostonian, ever become reconciled to the spectacle of the sun rising inland and setting over the ocean? That is what one has to put up with, in Brittany as in California. And the barnacles, which are as abundant on one side of the Atlantic as on the other, have in France no cutting edge; one may rub bare skin against them with impunity. And there is no seaweed —

not because it does not grow, but because it is all
promptly carted off, to be turned into a fertilizer.
How mountainously the stuff did come sweeping
into our little cove on the Massachusetts shore, and
how overpowering was its accumulated smell!
There was a time when we thought we could not
bear it, and must go home. Later, hardened by
habit, we could hardly bear a seashore without it;
and Breton beaches at first seemed curiously in-
sipid. I suppose that was a part of their unreality.
Pretty nearly incredible were the citified shrimp-
hunters, with their absurd costumes and their
little nets. A still funnier game is played by the
children, who go along the shore looking for cuttle-
fish; when they find one, they jab a hook into him
and pull him inside out. After all, that is a better
sport than collecting birds' eggs, as we used to do.
And stamps, and coins; but those were harmless
manias.

Every kind of collecting has become odious to
me now. It means slavery; and the bigger your
collection, the more tyrannical a master it is. Of
all philosophers, the one I most admire is that
ancient who owned only a drinking cup and threw
that away when he saw a man drinking out of his
hand. Even books, if you let them, will crowd you
out of house and home. And the accumulation of
data for future literary use is very likely to defeat
its own end. I once had a friend, a scholar of real

distinction, who started a card-catalogue. He had published several works of ripe learning, and people were already speaking of him as the coming man in his field of research. At this point his cabinet began to possess him. He could talk of little else. Never did he let slip an opportunity to lure colleagues to his study, that they might view his treasure and listen to the exposition of his system. The collection grew and grew, like the charitable Arab's camel. Many years that student lived, and every year found him more competent than the year before; but he never gave the waiting world any further proof of his competence. Card-catalogues, I am sure, were cast out of Erewhon, what time the oppressed inhabitants of that land arose in revolt and banished machines.

There were two hotels on that Breton beach where I spent a couple of summers with my family. It was a tiny village, but it could boast among its summer residents a scholar of note, a really first-rate man of letters, a political leader, and a poet-musician who won great renown as a *chansonnier*. This last celebrity was fond of attiring himself in the native costume, which the real natives never wore. On a small height he had planted his cottage, built of stone in the shape of a miniature castle, with tin battlements. A friendly chap, though; he gave his photograph to each of my children. But I must not forget my two hotels. One was modern and just a bit pretentious, frequented (as I eventually discovered) by people of aristocratic antecedents or aspirations. The other was old, unassuming, rather untidy, a resort of artists, writers, and other bohemians. A guest had painted on the dining-room door a lifelike and nearly life-size portrait of the proprietor, who was a delicious cook. Installed (for hygienic reasons) in the more elegant hostelry, I began to observe there a curious frigidity among the inmates, every group being apparently afraid of making acquaintance with some one of an inferior stratum. Yet they were all French; in England one is used to such an attitude. Very promptly I became a pariah, because I had in the place three friends who frequently called on me, and all three of them were Socialists. Although they were all men of means, with summer residences of their own, their proper place, of course, was in the cheaper inn. In the course of the season each of these establishments gave a concert — a Radical concert at the more modest house, a Reactionary concert at ours, with the patriotic *chansonnier* and his wife as stars and the local clergy as guests. Both entertainments were pretty good; I attended both, and contributed to both the antagonistic charities which were represented.

A curious incident of my sojourn in Brittany was the reading of *John Bull's Other Island*, in French garb, at the house of one of the Socialistic three. He was a great admirer of Shaw, whose works he was translating; indeed, he gave for two years a course on Shaw at the Sorbonne. For him, the dramatist was primarily a social reformer, only incidentally a humorist or satirist. The particular piece chosen for the occasion was selected because it so well exemplified the Irishman's views. It was excellently translated, the Irish brogue being rendered by a Breton type of French; and a professional actor from Rennes had been imported to do the reading. To my regret, that reading was never finished. The host, Mr. H., editor of a leading Socialist journal, had invited to the party as many Socialists as he could gather in the neighborhood, among them Mr. D., the Socialist mayor of a considerable city. Had our host forgotten that reformers never agree? Midway in the performance a discussion arose with regard to Shaw's intention: did the author advocate collective or individual exploitation? Mr. H., who held for collectivism, maintaining that the gigantic trusts of the United States are the next best thing to Socialism, naturally attributed that view to Shaw; while Mr. D., an individualist and a supporter of the small farmer, could see in the play nothing but individualistic doctrine. Each interpretation was based on the postulate that Shaw, being all-wise, must agree with the interpreter. In fact, Shaw presently dropped out of the debate altogether. "After all, our Breton peasants, each working for himself, do live!" cried D. "Under your system there would be a livelihood only for the most competent." "They have no business to live, in such misery and degradation," retorted H. "Better that they should perish and make way for a higher standard." Habitually gentle as doves, the opponents had by this time worked themselves into a frenzy. On H.'s neck the veins swelled until I thought they would burst; D.'s face was red as the reddest sunrise. "Let them live!" shouted D. "Let them die!" shrieked H. At that, D. and his retainers rose and left the house. And all that summer the D. family and the H. family, previously closest of friends, would not speak to each other.

For a while, I feared the altercation would go on as long as an old-fashioned baseball game. I remember one match, on a Fourth of July, between two rustic teams, not far from Worcester. I, as a "city feller," and therefore supposedly conversant with all the rules of the sport, had been asked to serve as umpire. Early in the day the contest began; up and up rose the score, like stocks in the recent boom. From morn to noon they played, from noon to dewy eve, a summer's day. Just a few minutes off for luncheon. Towards four p.m., one of the catchers having become disabled, I took his place and caught behind the bat, still continuing my function as umpire. When darkness finally parted the contestants, the score was eighty-six to sixty-eight.

Those summer days! The sweet relaxation of them, the sense of irresponsible freedom! Best of all, perhaps, the days when summer is in the offing, when we are still looking forward to it, when we sniff it in the air. I never smell violets without recalling some scene of early spring in Paris, where boys are selling bunches of those flowers in the streets. In the era of bustles, a fashionably clad young woman goes wagging her way along the sidewalk; and an urchin, as she passes, sacrifices his whole remaining stock of violets for the fun of depositing it on her rear platform and seeing her strut on, unconscious of her load. As she pursues her course, other *gamins* contribute their mite — a package of licorice pastilles, an empty corset-box, a mangy *ouistiti*; and still she struts, in happy ignorance, all through the Chaussée d' Antin.

Violets and horse-chestnut blossoms — markers of the season when opera relaxes and Madame Marchesi used to hold the closing exercises of her singing classes. One of these I recall distinctly, having been invited by one of her pupils, a powerful young contralto, who on that occasion sang "O mio Fernando." There I saw the Baron Haussmann, refashioner of Paris, famous for his dealings in real estate and his fondness for ladies of the theatre: a tall, high-shouldered, bony man, clean-shaven, with keen eyes and a broad smile. There, too, was that alienist whom I had met in Florence. But he deserves a separate paragraph.

It was a large *pension* in the north of Florence. One of the houses which composed it had been the dwelling of George Eliot when she was preparing to write *Romola*. It was kept by and for Americans, a very satisfactory home, if one wished to fraternize with compatriots. Of these it offered a sufficient variety, among them a wealthy lunatic and his keeper. The patient, a dark, rather portly man of thirty-five or forty, always quiet and unassuming, exhibited no peculiarity save persistent silence. For this defect the alienist, his guardian, made ample amends. I believe he was a specialist of some repute. A man in his seventies, I should say, voluble, suave, the pink of dandyism. Not only did his extensive wardrobe conform to the latest dictates of fashion; he even surpassed the style. His extraordinarily high collar, for example, was fastened both at the bottom, where other collars are buttoned, and at the top, with two huge diamond studs. Precious stones of Oriental magnificence gleamed from his shirt front and from the rings that covered his fingers. Always immaculately neat, with a perfect shave. For some reason he chose to make a confident of me, although I was only twenty. Many were the conferences we held.

Suspicious at first, I found, as time went on, no motive but a desire for sympathy in his dilemma. You see, he was in love. In fact, he was engaged to a young Englishwoman; and his relatives were doing their level best to break off the match, alleging that his betrothed was a mercenary schemer, who wanted to marry him only for his money — which, I judged, was abundant. Dreadful stories they told him about her; but one glance into her sweet face and her pure eyes was enough to refute all their slanders. Of course, she loved him for himself alone. Didn't I think so? You will agree that my position was a difficult one. I could not help thinking that healer and patient might advantageously have exchanged places. How did it come out? I believe the cruel relatives ultimately won the day, contriving to put the fair adventuress into jail for some previous adventure. This much I inferred from rather broken remarks when I saw him again. His love never got beyond its spring-time: no Indian Summer for him — not even a June.

June links itself not only with love and flowers and baseball, but also with Jules Verne; for on a hot, sunny day of that month I made his acquaintance. A memorable occasion; all the details are stamped on my memory. An awning over the window, sounds of the street rising muffled by their climb of three stories. It is a little hotel on Washington Street, near Dover Street, in Boston. We are

halting there in process of migration. On the centre-
table lies a thick, red-covered volume, which I for
days have refused to touch, stupidly mistaking it
for a scientific report. *A Journey to the Centre of
the Earth*; hardly has boredom impelled me to open
it, when the pictures reveal something of its magic.
Forevermore June shall recall those never-to-be-
forgotten figures — the eccentric uncle, the unwilling nephew, and Hans, the imperturbable
Icelandic guide.

They emerged, you remember, on Stromboli,
having been spewed out from the earth's interior.
As I read of that marvelous outcoming, I never
dared to imagine that I should ever behold Stromboli, however hot my secret desire. But I have seen
it, by day and night. The first time was on an
Italian steamer, an old boat, but scrubbed so clean
that one could have eaten off her deck anywhere;
and the food so delicious that one could have eaten
it off the ground. There was an uncommonly large
crew, under uncommonly good discipline. The
captain, a fat, good-natured man, certainly did not
look the part of a martinet, but he ruled his ship.
I fancy nothing escaped his notice. As we were
going aboard, a lady passenger remarked softly to
her companion: "Dear me! I wish we had some
peaches!" The captain, not far away, said nothing; but I saw him call a cabin-boy and whisper
something in his ear. And just before the gang-

plank was hauled away, the lad came bounding aboard with a crate of peaches in his arms. We had a batch of missionaries with us. A pair of them, on their way to India, had a very pretty and very precocious little child, whom everyone admired. As it was toddling about the deck, the captain suddenly blew his whistle. We all started. Instantly the mate and the bo's'n appeared, and saluted. "Boys," said the captain, "I want you to see that baby!"

So we passed Stromboli. I never reached its ruddy top, nor do I believe it offers nocturnal hospitality. And I fancy the clouds that envelop its summit are all of its own making.

OUT OF ANTIQUITY

I HAVE been recording a good many impressions of Paris, but they are all — or nearly all — recent ones. My accessible store, however, on which I hope to draw now that I am not likely ever to acquire any new stock, is drawn from a constantly aging antiquity. When I first knew Paris, in 1875, the Avenue de l'Opéra was still only in contemplation, although the Opera itself was already built and functioning. In fact, my first experience of grand opera — a performance of *Faust* — was in that house. I wondered then, and have never ceased to wonder, at the abuse which allows *ouvreuses* to disturb the audience with their chatter and clatter over the seating of late arrivals. To an American, the *ouvreuses* seem an unnecessary institution, anyhow. Equally needless and exasperating seems the obligation to pay for a program, an additional source of noise and confusion when people come in. In our country the program is paid for by advertising; whereas in France, in the lesser theatre, the advertisements, with a few jokes, are displayed on the drop curtain — surely a more efficacious exhibit.

I am trying to visualize Paris as it was without its main artery. There was nothing to precede it.

When the Avenue first came into existence (as I learn from an old print) it was lined with trees. That is quite in accord with the semi-bucolic quiet of the Paris of 1875. The advent of the automobile has transformed the whole tone of life. The streets, even then, seemed crowded and noisy; but we simply did not know what noise and crowd are. Convenient as the taxi is, we have lost something precious in the vanishing of the old two-story, horse-drawn omnibus. I believe I have never known another mode of transportation as fascinating as a ride on the *impériale* of an omnibus. Nothing escaped you, and nothing jarred you; and you always arrived at your destination quite as soon as you wanted to arrive there. A good long route was to be preferred, stretching nearly all the way across Paris and covering both sides of the river. There used to be a bus labeled "Panthéon — Place Something-or-Other" in the north of the city, which was still to be read on buses years after the Place Something-or-Other itself had disappeared. About the old routes there was a fixity which inspired confidence and constantly reviewed memories. Fresh air, a commanding outlook, a diversified and always interesting view, a progress quick enough for exhilaration but not too quick for inspection, a comfortable seat, a modest fare, a safe and sure arrival: these were the advantages of the *impériale* — advantages never to be offered by any other means of transportation. The passing of the *impériale* is one of life's irreparable losses.

Another type of degeneration is to be found in the *Guignol*. I do not mean, of course, the *Grand Guignol*, which in the good old days was happily unborn. I am referring to the regular ancient Punch and Judy show, ecstatic delight of children and sedate joy of the mature. One still sees the puppet stages on the Champs Élysées, in the gardens of the Tuileries and the Luxembourg, but one misses the glad shrieks of the juvenile audience; and, wondering why, one takes a strangely uncomfortable bench under the trees. But what does one behold? After an unconscionable wait, the curtain goes up — not to the well-known, reliable performance, but to something new and pointless. There is no Judy, no baby, no Jack Ketch, no doctor; there is very little banging of wooden heads. One might almost as well be at a grown-up theatre. And there is continual irritating supervision, to prevent unpaid presence and intrusion under the ropes. It really does not seem worth while. After one experiment, in 1931, I did not venture it again.

As to the little grown-up theatres themselves, they seem happily to have suffered no radical change — the Théâtre Cluny, for instance. The plays are new, but there is no newness in the stuff of which they are made. Gone are the actors of my boyhood, but the present artists have evidently learned their art in the good old school. If there is nothing quite equal to the former Variétés, there is good entertainment still to be had there; and last year's revival of *La Vie parisienne* at the Mogador could not easily be surpassed in any age. Indeed, in one of the Mogador performers I recognized a former star of the Variétés; only, instead of a *jeune premier*, as he used to be, he was now an elderly foreign baron, and he was as good in the one rôle as in the other.

At the Opéra, the Opéra comique, and the Mogador — perhaps at many other houses — they have an excellent arrangement for the *location* of your seats in advance, when on Monday morning you go to make your choice for the week. To prevent crowding, there are two box-offices instead of one, each intended for half of the week's evenings and *matinées*, and each plainly labeled to that effect. Getting one's tickets is now an easy and expeditious process. I remember when, at the Comédie française, one had to give one's name and wait for a ticket to be written out. Even now one is subjected, on entering the show, to the delay of the double exhibition of the ticket — the *contrôle*, as it is called. Long waits are still customary before the curtain and between the acts; but there are interesting promenades, and often enticing refreshments. I was surprised to find, last year, that the worst offender in time-wasting was the good old Odéon, which also has least accommodation for passing the time thus wasted.

Ancient memories, however, are not confined to Paris. Only this last winter I paid a reminiscent visit to Dorchester, Mass., my native town. The house where I was born is no longer there, but I can visualize it, rather vaguely, and I can find the spot where it stood. One of my earliest recollections is the act of picking up bits of thread from the sitting-room carpet and stowing them in an open-work ornament at the top of the stove, under the idea that I was a fisherman depositing captured fish in a basket. I wonder how, at that age, I possessed so much technical knowledge; apparently, however, I did not know that the fisherman's basket is chronically empty — a fact which later experience obtruded on my consciousness. Another of the very first Dorchester pictures represents myself, beside the piazza, gazing in wonder at a large toad. Toads continued to be objects of my admiration; I was in the habit of fondling them at a later Dorchester period of my existence, when I was seven or so and lived in a different quarter. I loved their beautiful eyes; and I never ceased to wonder at the rapidity with which they secured their prey, darting out a long, sticky tongue at any small, moving object and precipitating it into their capacious interior. Of the endless capacity of that interior I made a test during a whole afternoon, which I devoted to incessant offering of live bait, without the slightest indication of repletion. Buddha-like was the tireless, undisturbed serenity of the devouring idol, with its rounded belly and its unchanging smile. As to the prevalent belief that toads "give you warts," I amply refuted that superstition by experience. With all my daily handling of the maligned creatures, I never had a wart until I was a grown man and was living in Paris, where no such source of infection was accessible. I then, after various vainly gentle methods, got rid of the unwelcome excrescence by burning it out with a red-hot poker — a cure which, despite its efficacy, I cannot conscientiously recommend.

The earliest Dorchester pictures, as they return to my eye, are evidently not direct impressions, but the result of recollection and subsequent visualization; for I always see in them my own diminutive form. That must be a sure proof that the image is not direct; it is evidence, also, of the persistence and the clearness of the first impression, even into a period of childhood when the secondary production could be made. That period was presumably the time of my second Dorchester residence, during which Dorchester was annexed to Boston. I remember sitting on a big, smooth stone which stood at the corner of School Street and the "Upper Road," and meditating seriously on the

responsibilities incurred by that annexation. Close
to that junction was Squire Vose's grocery store,
where I used to go to get a "east cake." And right
beside the grocery store one got a beautiful view of
Boston Harbor, which startles me every time I revisit Dorchester. One doesn't expect it at all; but
the land is high, and no tall buildings intervene; all
of a sudden the blue sea flashes upon you. On the
Upper Road, now Washington Street, ran a horse-
car line, passing by Grove Hall and entering the
city. The fare for little children was only three
cents. On the first day of the week I used to board
the car, armed with a silver or a nickel three-cent
piece (we then had three-cent pieces of both types,
although the silver one was inconveniently small),
and bound for Sunday School. I valued Sunday
School especially for the opportunity it offered to
borrow books from the library. Besides, I was very
fond of the pastor, who one day read aloud to us
"The Ancient Mariner," in imitation of Edwin
Booth, whose rendering of the poem he had once
heard. I liked my teacher, too, and I liked to meet
the other boys of my class. One of these, a boy
whose eyes were a bit slanting, we nicknamed "the
heathen Chinee," and we were cruelly fond of
quoting from our geography book the sentence:
"The Chinese are but half civilized." The Sunday
School offered other delights: a Christmas tree,
with presents for all; occasional private theatricals;

ice cream parties; an annual picnic at Downer's Landing, in the Harbor. Downer's Landing, as I remember it, was rather a dreadful place, in spite of some swings; it was littered with papers, orange peel, and watermelon rinds — evidence of previous picnics. One had to be very careful where one sat down.

Though born on the "Lower Road" I have always identified myself with the "Upper Road," which ran from Grove Hall out to Dr. Means's church, and beyond, out into the mysterious distance, toward Milton. In that remote faerie-land, my father, my mother, and I occasionally used to picnic, at the top of a field that sloped down to the blue curves of the Neponset River. Surprising it is, but true, that the blue color vanished as you approached the water. Similarly shy of approach was the blueness of the Blue Hills. I have long, in my mind, associated the Blue Hills with the Blue Alsatian Mountains — I dare say because I first heard that song when, at the age of fifteen or so, I was calling on some old Blackstone friends on Blue Hill Avenue. I still recall the name of the girl who sang it, a chance visitor whom I had never seen before and never saw again, although I subsequently heard that she became a very active and beneficent physician.

On the "Upper Road," opposite School Street, was a factory where silverware was made — the "silver factory," we called it; a dominating and apparently immutable feature of the neighborhood. Yet one day, to everyone's astonishment, an explosion was heard, the air was full of fragments, and the factory had vanished. The boiler, which was to blame for all, was found half-way down the grassy hillside, an eighth of a mile away. It seems the disaster occurred at the noon hour, when all the workers were absent, except one watchman, who, warned in time, saved himself by jumping from a window. Such an event cannot fail to disturb, in a child, the infantile static conception of life. For me, a personally disturbing influence was the habit I had formed of visiting the establishment daily, to grind a point on the end of a nail of which I was trying to make a certain toy — a sort of ice-pick. Fortunately my habitual hour was not the hour of the disaster. Quite personal was the behavior of a long board from the factory, which, after an aerial flight, descended and planted itself like a stake in our front garden — an unquestionable distinction for our household.

That garden was the scene of an unfortunate horticultural experiment due to my father's unfamiliarity with New England flora (he was bred in Philadelphia and had long resided in Alabama). He and I, both close observers and enthusiastic experimenters, had noticed in a field a strange plant with beautiful purple flowers and pretty berries. Wishing to cultivate a thing of such attractiveness, we dug it up and proudly planted it in our little garden. What a fall our pride suffered when a well-informed neighbor told us that the plant was deadly nightshade! To give a bad name is apparently as fatal to a plant as to a dog; at any rate, it banished ours. Another capture of ours, in the same field, was the imprisonment, in a round collar-box, of a peculiarly big and formidable spider, which had displayed its black and yellow bulk in a widespread web. To approach the web closely and to bring together the top and the bottom of the old-fashioned collar-box in such a way as to enclose the unsuspecting spider, was an act not devoid of excitement, especially as we did not know how poisonous the creature might be. Its evil disposition, at any rate, did not seem to interfere with its serene acceptance of captivity. Having spun a broad new web, it devoted itself to the capture of domestic flies with the same zeal it had shown in the pursuit of the field variety; and so it happily lived until its peaceful demise. Another excursion into the domain of science was our attempt to domesticate tadpoles. These we caught in a little pool in an old quarry, and brought home triumphantly in a jar. Our first attempts were unsuccessful. The pollywogs, to sustain their fragile life, required a daily change of water; and the aqueous discharge from our kitchen faucet did not meet their needs. Not until we replenished their jar by a daily trip to their native quarry could we induce them to live. But what a joy was the spectacle of their development when at last we learned how to overcome their fastidious aversion! To see the sprouting of one pair of legs, then another, and the disappearance of the now incongruous tail, what a joy to the heart of the paternally-minded scientist! And what a reward it was to see our *protégés* actually jumping! For jump they did, as long as we kept them in captivity, and presumably forever after their liberation.

The blowing up of the silver factory was not the only sensational explosion that I associate with the "Upper Road." On that same road, nearly opposite School Street, and therefore close to the ill-fated factory, were two big, fine residences belonging to a Mr. G. The owner had built one for himself and the other, just like it, for his son, who was about to be married. But the son died on the eve of the wedding, and the father, unwilling that the new dwelling should ever be occupied by anyone else, insisted on leaving it empty. There it stood, then, beside Mr. G.'s house, desolate and decaying, to the general disapproval of the neighbors, who condemned such wastefulness. Mr. G., however, was a rich man, who could do as he liked. Having a considerable garden and barn as well as his dwelling, he needed a number of servitors. Chief among these was a certain Mr. W., who lived in a comfortable house near by, on the little lane just across the way from School Street. His three children, Peter, Nellie, and Tad, by virtue of proximity, were among my most familiar playmates. The whole family, indeed, was well known and much respected. A favorite game, among us children, was hide-and-seek in Mr. G.'s big barn, wherein our most beloved passage was through a trap-door which we called the "scoot-hole" — presumably a distortion, by popular etymology, of an Irish workman's pronunciation of "scuttle." At any rate, "scoot-hole" it was for us, and one of the stable institutions of our lives. Then, without any warning, came the crash. There came weekly to our house a washerwoman, who, in addition to her function as laundress, served as gazette of the town. On that particular Monday she had news to retail so startling as to seem almost incredible. It appeared that Mr. W. for years had been pilfering from Mr. G., and at last had been discovered; the employer, however, in his kindness, had not caused the arrest of Mr. W., but had simply discharged him from his service. Thus was the world upset. Vanished from my life were Peter, Nellie, and Tad; vanished the barn and the delectable "scoot-hole." For a while life seemed scarcely worth living. In my dreams I could hear Peter's familiar stutter (he did stutter pretty badly), but

I was nevermore to hear it in reality, although we attended the same school; doubtless he was in a higher class than I.

It was the Gibson School, on School Street — a grammar school, and I was in the primary department. I went to look at it, when I visited the old haunts, last spring. A large brick building had been erected in the yard, where we used to play; but the old schoolhouse stood intact behind it. Looking in through a window, I could see the very room where I learned the multiplication table, under the ministration of Miss Tinker. I could almost hear again the infantile voices reciting in chorus: "Two tums one is two, two tums two is four, two tums three is six" and so on until the culminating "Two tums twelve is twenty-four." Why did everything stop with *twelve*? One of the many insoluble and eternal mysteries of life. Another unchanging mystery was the division of every mental arithmetic example into two symmetrical parts. With mental arithmetic I am leaping to a much more advanced stage of my scholastic existence. An unchanging formula regulated its conduct. "If one apple costs three cents, what will ten apples cost? Ten apples will cost ten tums three cents, which is thirty cents. *Answer*: If one apple costs three cents, ten apples will cost ten tums three cents, or thirty cents." It was always a relief when one reached the second half of the formula, the part labeled "answer"; this word, indeed, became a symbol of the known and therefore easy. We used to shout it with gleeful loudness. But we had to guard carefully against any deviation from regularity in the supposedly mechanical half of the problem. If we omitted a word, or changed any phrase, in the formula, it was wrong, and the whole performance was a failure. At times, arithmetical computation was assisted by an abacus, a strange machine which the teacher would produce from a drawer.

Aside from arithmetic, we had spelling and some simple reading. Why did we so love to gnaw away the pasteboard corners of our poor little books? They had neither flavor nor nutriment. As to the consumption of slate-pencil dust, that pleasure was confined to the girls, who also were the devourers of pickled limes — both of these delicacies being despised by the boys. We all united, however, in "lozengers," purchased at the corner "store"; "sassyfras" was perhaps the favorite. "Liquorish," also, was a delight, either the "stick" or the "root." Gum-drops and "jaw-breakers" were generally beyond our means. I do not remember that any of us, at that time, were addicted to chewing-gum, which came at a later stage of our development, at the age of marbles, tops, and ball. Our sports, at the Gibson School, were mainly tag and catch.

Woe unto the boy who appeared with any new article of clothing! The offending apparel had to be initiated: if it were a hat, it had to be crushed; boots were stamped on; clothes were soiled and, if possible, torn. Such was the custom of those young savages. On one unhappy day my kind and unsuspecting mother sent me to school newly arrayed. During the recreation period — or, as we called it, the "*re*cess" — it occurred to her to look in at the school to see how I was faring. It was a rainy day, and the soil was wet and filthy. As she entered the yard, she saw a heap of youngsters piled upon the ground in the middle of the enclosure; and, looking for her darling boy, she discovered him, bedraggled and more or less lacerated, at the bottom of the semi-human mass. My mother was a lady of uncommon sweetness and dignity; but this spectacle was too much for her, and she fiercely charged the crowd with her umbrella, scattering the frightened little rowdies like chaff before the wind. My mother made vigorous representations to Mr. Endicott, the headmaster. I believe I never was annoyed again.

There were lovely days in the spring, when the great sloping field beyond the "Upper Road" was clothed in fresh green, and newly appeared brooklets went coursing down the hill. Braving the peril of wet feet, we could then explore our new territory. There were happy days in the autumn, too, when my father and I would go a-nutting and bring home a rich harvest of hickory-nuts and chestnuts. "Pignuts" were not worth eating; and butternuts were both rare and distressingly oily. Beechnuts we did occasionally secure. In the late summer there were fields entirely covered with goldenrod — great golden seas, above which a child's head would barely emerge. Winter would supply snow-forts and various elaborate structures of snow and ice. One of these, engineered by Peter and me, near his house, was reinforced with brick, held together by mud instead of mortar. My family lived in a house of the type the English call "semi-detached" — that is half of a double house, commodious and convenient, except that the cellar had a habit of becoming flooded in the spring. I remember one season — peculiarly delightful to me — when my father and I had to construct a raft to convey us from the foot of the cellar stairs to the furnace. My mother did not enjoy these Noah-like episodes, which she regarded as conducive to rheumatism. She did, however, enjoy the winter evenings of wind and storm, when the wind would howl about the house, and she (being of a somewhat romantic temperament) would like to imagine that we were in a chalet on the Alps. It was at this time that I made myself, out of waste white paper and some pins, a note-book, wherein I purposed to record all the new words I should acquire in my reading. This vocabulary, I am sorry to say, never extended beyond the first entry: "Mariner, one who sails over the sea," which I have always associated with our adventures in the flooded cellar. In dry seasons the cellar was used by my father for the fabrication of toys for me, some of which kept their utility for years. There was a large attic in which I could play, and there was a woodshed which sometimes witnessed scenes best left unrecorded. Near by was a large, pretentious house with a "cupolo," inhabited by a wealthy shoe-dealer, who had a little son. This boy would occasionally (glad occasions!) take us into his vegetable garden, where we would dig potatoes and bake them in the embers of a "bomfire." I can guess why we said "bomfire"; but I have never been able to divine the reason of our pronunciation "carpender," of which, even now, it is hard to divest myself. How delicious those baked potatoes were! Nothing else was quite so good, except — possibly — the raw carrots we sometimes extracted from a barrel in a neighboring barn, whose owner (we firmly believed) willingly permitted this liberty.

One painful episode obtrudes itself when I turn back to the very beginning of our residence on School Street. I had been sent out to purchase a dozen eggs at a "grocery store" — not Squire Vose's but a more distant one. Returning, with the eggs in a paper bag, I noticed, across the street, an elderly lady walking in my direction. For some reason, I had an insane fear of being kidnaped, and an old woman, of however respectable appearance, was an object of terror. Perhaps Horatio Alger's *Tattered Tom* was partly responsible for my folly. I hastened my steps; but, not succeeding in distancing my innocent imaginary pursuer, I broke into a run and, jolting my bag, broke one of the eggs. I reached home, then, breathless and excited, and minus one egg. My mother told me subsequently that shortly after my arrival the old lady, having noticed my perturbation, called to assure my mother that she was perfectly harmless, being, in fact, particularly fond of children. Even this humiliating experience, and my mother's ridicule, did not entirely cure me of my fear. I remember once fleeing from an old woman, in Boston, in a back alley off Brookline Street, although I was in company with another child, who did not entirely share my apprehension. Much as I should like to consign it to oblivion, I cannot forget my theatrical greeting to my mother: "You might never have seen your little boy again!"

OLD HAUNTS

WHEN no anniversaries are available, a revisit to old places will sometimes revive memories. I have just been walking through Brookline Street and the adjacent neighborhood. We used to live there, in a corner house; and for some time, having let a part of our home to the Gibbses, we took our meals in a select establishment next door.

"It says here in the paper," said the boarding-table humorist, an agreeable young man whose name I have forgotten (if I ever knew it), "that Charley Grandgent was seen this afternoon promenading on Brookline Street with a flaxen-haired young lady." The young person in question certainly was flaxen-haired, and her flaxen hair hung down her back; and her name was Lizzie L. Her family not only ate but roomed in that house. I suppose she and I were about five years old. I was not at all disturbed by the journalistic publicity, but she declared we must be married at once. Her family's domestic position facilitated the rapid execution of her project, which she proceeded to carry out, unaided. I cannot recall that I made any active resistance, although I must have protested inwardly. Her father's Sunday suit was taken from a closet and hung on the back of a chair, to serve as minister; she improvised a wedding service, and performed all the parts. My only function was to receive a ring, which I obediently put on. It was a ring which she herself had made from a lot of little beads strung on a thread. Despite a removal of my family to Dorchester, I kept the token for several years, until it wore out. Our marriage evidently was not announced, for I lost no caste among the children of the vicinity.

I do not believe even Tracy Gibbs heard of it. Tracy was the son of the people who occupied half of our domicile, and he was the most venerable of my playmates, having attained the mature age of ten. I used to wonder anxiously whether I should ever achieve that longevity. It gave me great satisfaction to repeat, over and over, "Tracy, ten; Tracy, ten," and to marvel at the manifest predestination implied in the alliteration. It was a matter of some solicitude that my name never would alliterate with "ten" nor even rime with it.

Gazing on Brookline Street, I can recall even earlier promenades on that sidewalk in feminine company. For there my kind Irish nurse, Mary, used to wheel me in my perambulator. I can still see that modest black vehicle. But I cannot bring back the face of the nurse, although I know she was comely and good; my mother thought very highly of her.

On the neighboring Sharon Street, where most of my playmates lived, housekeeping was sometimes quietly, though quite illegally, conducted by Gertie L. and me, in the service entrance under the front stoop of her house. Nearly all the houses in that vicinity had such a little vestibule. Gertie used to bring out of the house tiny and very thin slices of bread, spread, in default of butter, with moistened crumbs of cake. It was a thrilling experience.

There was another little girl — quite mature, for she was ten or so — of whom my mother had a high opinion. So high, indeed, that once she allowed her to borrow me for a day (I being then about four years of age) and take care of me at her home. I can remember that she gave me a very happy outing. She lived nearby, on Washington Street. Only a few months ago I saw in the paper a notice of the death of Mabel, who in the meantime had become a writer of some distinction. Her daughter I met, several years since, at Radcliffe College, where she was a graduate student.

Right opposite our house lived little Carrie (I have quite forgotten her last name), who was justly renowned for her good behavior and her polite manners. My mother held her up as a model. Carrie was good company, too — not a bit of a prig.

If Lizzie L. was conspicuous for her flaxen hair, what shall I say of the radiant golden hair of Edith T., as applauded for her beauty as Carrie for her character? She must have been really very pretty indeed, but she had lost most of her good looks when I saw her later in life. As a child, she did not seem at all puffed up by her charm nor by the magnificence of her dwelling; for she and her brother Harry lived in one of those imposing houses with an abnormally high flight of front steps. There was a block of them, not far along from the humbler abodes that we inhabited.

Speaking of magnificence, was there ever quite the equal of Chester Square, with its fountain of goldfishes? What lofty, high-studded houses, and what sedate quiet in that lordly realm! And to think it is now only a part of Massachusetts Avenue, and the fishes are all departed!

I once lived for a while in West Chester Park, close to Chester Square. But this was at a later epoch, when I was nine or ten. A little boy, even younger, lived in the same house, and I had the unprecedented experience of being admired for my age and my mature talents. This little boy especially admired my drawing, of which I was, I fear, unduly proud. One day he brightened my life by asking me, entreatingly: "Will you teach me to draw?" The lessons began at once and lasted several weeks. I used to sketch figures for my pupil to copy; and if

he did not become a Raphael, it must have been
my fault. Perhaps, after all, I was really no
Perugino.

Not far from Chester Park, on Washington
Street, in the region known as "Boston Neck,"
there was a little, very modest family hotel, where
my family dwelt a while before moving to Brookline Street. Beside it, until very recently, one
could see a little alley where one day my father and
I came down out of the hotel to crack nuts on the
curb.

And close by, in a poor slum, lived the Lame
Boy. He was, and is still, for me, a very real and
intimate person, although I never spoke to him or
knew his name. As we walked through, — my
father and I, — we used to see him sitting in a
noisome back yard, a crutch lying beside him; that
was the sum of my actual acquaintance with the
Lame Boy, yet I used to recognize him with the
affection normally bestowed on a dear friend. I
have come to the conclusion that I must have con-
fused him, in my mind, with the Lame Boy in some
story that had been read to me. I suppose I was
about three, and did not do much independent
reading as yet. But I knew that story-book Lame
Boys are always pathetic and generally ingratiat-
ing; and these appealing characteristics I transferred unhesitatingly to the Lame Boy of Boston
Neck, who, beyond any manner of doubt, had ex-

perienced all the sorrows that had afflicted the
Lame Boy of the story-books. I never could see
him, in his sordid surroundings, without a loving
smile and a gush of tears. Even now, when I pass
that spot, transformed as it is, I feel a pang and a
choking sensation, and involuntarily I look about,
on the east side of Washington Street, for my old
favorite. If he is still alive, he must be a Lame
Boy of some eighty-five or ninety.

When I look, nowadays, at children of three or
so, I wonder whether they can have as many feel-
ings and thoughts as I had at that age. It doesn't
seem possible, but one can't be really sure. My
tiniest grandchildren, impassive though they appear, may be in the midst of a rich emotional and
intellectual existence. Fear is no doubt a familiar
sensation. For a while I could not go to sleep until
my mother had promised me to go to bed in "a
quarter of an hour and twenty minutes," the
"twenty minutes" seeming to me then a small
fragment of "a quarter of an hour." At that same
timorous bedtime she had to assure me that she
knew I should never have St. Vitus' dance, I
having been horribly shocked by the sight of that
malady in the person of a lady at our boarding-
house. For a considerable period, before I would
go to sleep, my poor mother was obliged to affirm
her certitude that I should never be insane nor
have St. Vitus' dance. Other things, not terrify-

ing, were endlessly puzzling. Life was full of tiresome mysteries. Why, for instance, did one say, at table: "yes, *if you please*," but "no, *I thank you*"? The two polite formulas seem to signify the same thing, but are not at all interchangable. Then, one must remember, when asked one's age, to answer: "three and a half"; while, if questioned about the time of day, one must reply, "half-past three." This latter response is quite ridiculous (I never could see why) when applied to one's age. I observed, with wonder, that different classes of people have very different styles of holding their hands, as they walk along the street; indeed, I used to try to imitate them on the way to church. My mother, later in life, used to relate wise sayings of mine with which I often enlivened conversation at the boarding-house table. Somebody having observed that "the pleasures of anticipation are always greater than the pleasures of realization," I remarked: "Yes, I know that is true. Before I had my elephant, I thought it would make me perfectly happy; but, now that I have it, I find I am no happier than before." It was a toy elephant that nodded its head — enough to make any reasonable child happy, despite the dulness of satiety. I confess with shame that, although I could not be accused of being that hateful creature, an "infant phenomenon," I won considerable renown by the recitation of little poems. One of them, I remember, was the familiar masterpiece about "little drops of water, little grains of sand." Another, entitled "Where is God?" I declaimed with genuine feeling. I can still recall the thrill with which I responded:

> On the mountain, wild and high;
> In the sun, the moon, the sky;
> In the little birds that sing.
> God is found in everything.

My oratory may have been influenced by the example of my mother, who was an excellent reader, but I am sure that my expression was to a very considerable extent the reflex of my own feeling.

Even the commonplace "powers that be" were not without stirring effect. When I look down Canton Street and no longer see in its old conspicuousness the ancient police station which to us little children was an object of such awe, it seems to me that the world is incomplete. A memorable day for me was that on which my father was summoned to that office to answer to the charge of keeping a dog without a license. It was, I fear, all my fault. A stray dog, without collar, name, or home, insisted on adopting us, to the great delight of the youngest member of the family. My satisfaction was a little marred, to be sure, by his conduct the first night, when he, having been excluded from the house, filled the neighborhood with heart-rending whines and nearly scratched a hole through the back door. The next day, however, I paraded the street with him with renewed pleasure; and, when asked by a policeman whose dog that was, I proudly answered: "Mine." This colloquy was followed by the fearful call to the police station and, not long after, by the disappearance of our humble canine retainer. What happened to him, I never was told.

Perhaps it is time to quit this earliest stage and turn to words written in my memory, as Dante says, "under larger headings." Let us skip to the years when I was ten or eleven — quite as old as the Tracy Gibbs of Brookline Street. That was an epoch of travel, but I shall not attempt to enumerate my journeys. I might sing of Maine and my Uncle Joseph, of New Hampshire and the White Mountains, of Vermont and the Green Mountains, of central Massachusetts and my Aunt Maria, of western Massachusetts, where in a favorite game the participants, to choose partners, used to march around the hall, clapping their hands and singing:

> Come, Philander, let's be a-marchin',
> Every one his true love s'archin'.

No, I shall go further than New England, confining myself, however, to Chester, Pa., then a large country village, quite separate from Philadelphia, though not remote from it. I went first in the spring, with my father, to visit his mother, who lived in a little stone house at the corner of two streets. Not far away, my father's brother-in-law had a tobacco shop, with a real wooden Indian in front. His son, my cousin Charley, lived nearby. I think I still have a picture of him in uniform, for he was an officer in the Civil War. That family presently moved out West, and I lost track of them. My grandmother was then ninety-three and very deaf, so I did not become very intimate with her. But she was always kindly, and I became attached to her little house, where my father and I slept in an attic. I recall vaguely some stories I picked up there. One fragmentary novel was called *The Banker's Daughter*; the only thing in it that I can remember is an illustration wherein the prosperous banker, leaning easily against a mantelpiece, is shooting his daughter, whose matrimonial preference is at variance with his. The unforgettable thing about that murderous banker is his nonchalant pose. Of another novel I have forgotten the title, but I remember distinctly that, even in a mutilated form, it gave you your money's worth. A young lady of refinement and very small means has been invited to visit some very rich distant relatives at their elegant and extensive estate in the country. One day, looking from a back window of the house, she sees her uncle, in elegant frock-coat and stove-pipe hat, walking across the lawn, when suddenly he disappears mysteriously and inexplicably, to the great wonder and distress of the beholder. Not until many pages later do we get the clue to the puzzle. It seems the uncle is the chief of a band of counterfeiters, who have their lair underground, beneath that lawn, the entrance being made quite invisible. In the den is a gruesome machine called "the kissing stone," consisting of two huge flat blocks of stone one on the other in perfect contact and so constructed that the upper one can be lifted and then dropped into place again. Originally intended for the printing of false bills, it can be used also for the execution of members of the band suspected of treachery. One such summary punishment is narrated, and we are told how, when the great upper stone was again raised, "the crushed and mangled body had fallen into the vault below." Another chapter is entitled "Through Satan's Eyes." The sorely tried visitor, having been much interested in a picture, on her bedroom wall, of Satan in Council, is particularly puzzled by the strange aspect of Lucifer's eyes. She climbs, then, on a chair, to examine the peculiar features more closely, and in so doing lays her hand inadvertently on a spring on the side of the frame. Forthwith the curious eyes slide apart, leaving two small apertures through which one can look into the adjacent room. Availing herself of that opportunity, she sees, chained to the wall, a horrible, hideous monster, equipped, on each jaw, with a double row of teeth. Human the creature is, beyond doubt, but superhumanly repulsive. Not long after, waking up in the night, she sees this monster roaming about in her room. No explanation is obtainable from her uncle and aunt, who absolutely deny the existence of any such creature in the house. From an overheard conversation, however, she learns that it is the purpose of her host and hostess to marry her to this living nightmare. Meanwhile a potential hero has appeared, who, however, is soon consigned to the "kissing stone." How he ever escapes (for a hero must escape) is told, no doubt, in the lost final pages of the book. The extant portion ends with the opening of the stone jaws, to disclose nothing but emptiness. Very different is the tenor of another story, which I found in a book owned by the Chester Hotel, where my father, mother, and I spent the following summer. The subject of the tale has vanished from my mind, but I recall that its manner was mild, its scene was ancient provincial Jamestown, and its opening chapter revealed two gentlemen seated drinking together, near the shore, while one of them sings the praises of the month of October. The Chester Hotel itself was a mild and spacious wooden structure of very rural appearance. It was kept by a huge and powerful landlord of interesting conversation, who had two children: a boy of about my age, but

bigger and stronger, and a daughter still younger.
I liked the boy, and had pleasant companionship
with him, until the tragic happening which made
me a potential murderer. It happened in this wise,
with no previous warning. I was just entering a
doorway when the boy, who was hiding behind the
door, jumping out, threw a handful of flour into my
face, obscuring my sight. I, terribly frightened,
thought he had put out my eyes, and, in a frenzy
of rage, started after him, intending to do him some
mortal hurt. I overtook him on the stairs leading
down to the ground floor, and, in spite of his physical superiority, pulled him down and started to
choke him. Indeed, I might have succeeded in this
homicidal intent, had not his little sister, in fear,
run to her father and summoned his assistance. In
the course of the afternoon the unfortunate boy
knocked at the door of our apartment and apolo-
gized for his act. Even if prompted by his father,
his conduct was very handsome and destroyed the
last traces of my resentment. What remained and,
I hope, always will remain was terror at my angry
passion and its possible consequences. In fact, I
immediately resolved always to control my temper,
and strictly kept to that resolution for many years.
Thus, in part, may be explained the sweet disposition which has characterized me.

The boy and I became good friends again, and I
gladly consorted with another little lad, a friend

and neighbor of his, somewhat expert at sparring — or, as they called it, "fair fistin's." I have never met either of them again, nor have I again visited Chester, where I remember a little stone house said to have belonged to William Penn, the old Monitor, from which I carried off a rusty cannon-ball, and the Great Western, a twin ship to the Great Eastern.

All these things live in memory, though long vanished from my actual experience.